the wrong dog dream

the wrong dog dream

a true romance

§ Jane Vandenburgh §

COUNTERPOINT

BERKELEY

Author's Note on Technique
This is a work of nonfiction whose events verifiably happened.
I do, however, employ the techniques of fiction in recounting dialogue,
also in naming people and their dogs. I do this in order to avoid hurting
either their feelings or their reputations, as this was not my intent.
My intent, as always, is to get as close as I can to a truthful story.

Library of Congress Cataloging-in Publication is available.

ISBN 978-1-61902-120-4

Cover design by Natalya Bolnova
Interior design by David Bullen

COUNTERPOINT
1919 Fifth Street
Berkeley, CA 94710
www.counterpointpress.com

Printed in the United States of America
Distributed by Publishers Group West

10 9 8 7 6 5 4 3 2 1

for NOAH,
and for EVA,
children of our Wonder Years

contents

1
TRUE COMPANIONS

2
NEW WORLD DOG

3
WONDER YEARS

Love awoke, and life awoke.

LEO TOLSTOY, *War and Peace*
(translated by Richard Pevear and Larissa Volokhonsky)

1

true companions

You ask of my companions? Hills, sir,
and the sundown and a dog large
as myself... They are better than [human]
beings because they know but do not tell.

EMILY DICKINSON

friendship

Someone in my family dreamed it—no one now remembers who. The dream stems from something that happened when we were living in the East, and so begins in what feels solidly fact-based and actual:

Just back from a visit to Berkeley, we are stopping by the vets' to pick up our dog from boarding. We're all there—my husband, my daughter, my son, and me, all in that state of high alert known as "hypervigilance," all watching the door in the back of the waiting room. This is where the tech will appear, bringing our dog to us.

But here the dreamscape warps, time tilts, and everything starts to take too long: door opening, family standing, brought into slo-mo unison by their crazy love for this dog, an English springer spaniel named Whistler.

Now—as the dog is being led by the tech across the broad expanse of the tiled floor—the dreamer begins to get that something's a little off: that the two keep coming but remain very far away, that this family's fake, too loud, everyone saying false and scripted things—Hey, boy! There you are! We missed you, buddy! Come on! Come here! Good boy! like they are all repeating lines of cartoon dialogue.

Because this is not our dog—it only looks like him, a likeness in both appearance and behavior so uncanny that even the dog himself seems fooled, as this dog-who-is-not-our-dog comes wagging his no-tail rump at us, moving toward the strange family that now stands like a group of statues.

Only the dreamer notices what no one else yet sees: *That dog's a ringer!* the dreamer wants to say, somehow knowing—with a dreamer's spacious overview—how the mix-up came to be, that two lookalike dogs, so similar they might be clones, have been switched in grooming.

This is the wrong dog, the dreamer tries to say aloud to the tech. Our real dog's the one in back, but the dreamer's frozen and can't seem to get the words out and so must struggle again to speak, as the tech keeps leading this dog-who-is-not-our-dog across the waiting room.

The dreamer's now saying it more and more urgently, *Wrong dog! Wrong dog!* but locked together in the paralysis of sleep, lips, teeth, and tongue, all muscles of the dreamer's face, are stilled, words slurring as they're said—*wrrrrnng dwwwg, wrrrnnnn dwwwwggg*—so no one pays attention, and the dreamer now understands the true horror here, that what started as a loving, joyful dream has just become a nightmare.

❧ ❧ ❧

The whole neighborhood surrounding the vets' is called "Friendship," the word is used in a different way than you'd ever hear it said in California. Here it indicates place, in the sense of "township," from which you get that Friendship was the District neighborhood that had been settled by The Friends, also known as Quakers.

We got Whistler soon after we moved to Washington. We'd gotten a dog for many reasons, not the least among them our shared belief that—since a dog is the most earthbound of creatures—my having something land-based and terrestrial, who needed to be walked, would encourage me to get dressed and leave the house.

Because I'm a writer who works at home and can live so contentedly within the rooms of my mind, I do sometimes forget to walk outside. And I did really need to remember to go outside if I ever hoped to participate. I needed to participate or I'd never learn the first thing about this new place, nor would I meet anyone. I needed to meet people because we'd just moved to a town where I knew no one aside from the others in my family.

Our house was on Ordway Street near Connecticut in Cleveland Park in what was called—as I was finding out—the Second Alphabet. The street names in the Second and Third Alphabets have either two or three syllables, so two-syllable Ord-way might be reasonably found roughly halfway through the alphabet's second run-through. You could also deduce that Al-be-marle would lie so-and-so many blocks away, at the beginning of the Third.

Whistler's vet was on Bran-dy-wine.

If you studied the neat grid of the District map—as I compulsively did in trying to figure out how best to get from A to B—you'd notice that the broad state-named avenues, such as Massachusetts and Pennsylvania, would go wildly slashing through the four quadrants like sword slices cut by Zorro.

Friendship was right off Wisconsin's diagonal, right where the Third Alphabet streets, for no apparent reason, seemed to turn abruptly and run one way in the more inconvenient direction.

In order to get into the parking lot of the vet I always seemed to need to get extremely lost in several exploratory neighborhoods, then refind Wisconsin, then remember I needed to overshoot Brandywine in order to backtrack by driving any number of blocks down jagged alleyways. I'd started haunting the alleyways because a city possessing alleyways seemed like such an interesting luxury.

Driving the backside of the town's residential neighborhoods I'd feel this intoxicating mix of invisibility and stealth and minor criminality. I was also in a state of positive confusion, and because the District's laid out logically, I was beginning to get that my constant sense of being disoriented was likely sourced within me.

The problem was, I figured, I was simply not myself these days. We were moving to the East in stutter step, my husband, Jack, coming one year, me the next. And the year we got Whistler, my kids, then eleven and fifteen, were both still in California living with their father, having stayed behind to finish a year of school we all agreed was important.

But my kids being so far away left me feeling more than lonely; I felt almost depersonalized, as if I'd lost some major element in my sense of cosmic usefulness. I was also so habituated to the rhythms of the on-site maternal project that my body was still on automatic alert and would startle at three fifteen when it believed I belonged in one or another carpool pick-up lane.

Now, with no carpool assigned to me, I was driving aimlessly around, skirting the backyards of the empty houses of this lovely city filled with busy and important souls who'd all gone off to do their meaningful work, always coming upon another of my quaint discoveries: In a city where everyone works there'll be no one home in your neighborhood.

Do you know the trick of the alphabets? I'd ask some random person in a checkout line, to be met with the glazed eyes of someone who of course knows all about the alphabets.

And it wasn't just the offhand things I'd say, it was also my style in saying them, in that I'm friendly and easygoing, and this is a Topic Sentence kind of city, in which one sticks to the Talking Points.

I was now coming to understand what everyone else already knew: that time is actually *better than* money, in that they will *never* be enough of it. I was the only one I ever met in Washington who seemed to have time on her hands to be doing what I was doing, which was forever writing and rewriting that one same book time and time again.

And Jack and I were in our forties, too old—I was now deciding —to make new friends. What had I been thinking in agreeing to move to this place so far from my children, so far from all I knew?

I'd come to accompany the man I loved, in whose career I ardently believed, but there was also my own secret and selfish wish: I hoped to better understand California, where my family had lived for five generations, and was guessing I could do this best from what I now thought of as *exile*.

✗ ✗ ✗

But what did the dream mean, was it true that Whistler was changing from the easy, carefree puppy we'd expected when we got him, and how and why had this happened? Was it nature or nurture, or some mysterious combination, or was he simply growing into the dog he was always destined to become without regard for what Jack and I either had or had not done as owners?

Jack's always saying, Parents take too much credit and too much blame, and I will nod and nod, as if I agree, but this is actually my husband's theory, and it has almost nothing at all to do with my own worldview.

In my version of the way it works, I am *completely* in charge and so feel even *monumentally* responsible for everything that goes on with everyone. This derives from my own towering and all-encompassing maternity, my need to reflexively mother everyone, which is—and I do fully understand this—its own tiny psychological problem.

Which does not matter, as it all comes back to me. Know why? Because I'm The Mom Person.

✗ ✗ ✗

Maybe I was currently too sad to have a dog? Too depressed with the kids so far away to actually pay attention? And my two children being off in California was what I thought about obsessively. Was this somehow repetitive of the carelessness my two brothers and I endured at the hands of our own mom and dad, who were these, oh I will readily admit, these two charming, talented, highly attractive people, who were—let's face facts here—just such incredibly bad parents that they couldn't stick around to finish raising the three of us?

It made no difference that I knew my son and daughter were both safe, that their father and stepmother were doing a perfectly adequate job, that I understood that each of my kids was in the school where they wanted to be, with the same friends they'd had since preschool, that allowing them to stay in the West was recognizing the bonds of their friendships to be important. I was also trusting them in their autonomy, that is, their ability to get along without me.

Your friends? Almost nothing—I was now coming to understand —could matter more. Friends are so important that I was stunned to realize I'd just moved across the country from every friend I had ever had.

⚹ ⚹ ⚹

My kids were increasingly independent, they had their dad, their friends, their schools, they lived in their own hometown, but were they not now missing that most essential element of the happy childhood, their *mother?* in that you actually do need your own mom right there, hanging on your every word, as there's no one like your mom to witness your every thought and feeling and accomplishment? Isn't this, after all, what any good mother is meant for?

So if something was going wrong with our dog, then I—as the maternal element in this domestic setup—was obviously to blame.

If Whistler was turning out to be quirky or ill at ease, wasn't this simply a reflection of my own feelings about not fitting in? If he needed to be socialized to other animals, I was at fault, as I just didn't *know* anyone to go dogwalking with. So here was this pup who'd started life as two warm and fluffy handfuls of the purest joy turning out to have what the kids were now calling "Whistler's Issues."

It was true that this dog of ours now seemed strangely nervous and skittish. Our dog arrived as a sweet-natured puppy, but by the time he was half grown he had become such a fearful mass of jitters that the people we were getting to know would often remark on it, Whistler turning out to be what Jack called "a little tightly wrapped."

Okay, so maybe he was a little high-strung to begin with, then maybe in the unfair lottery he gets this writer-type person who is simply gazing off vacantly so much of the time. You don't mean to, it's just that as a writer you're so often driving imaginary streets and roads instead of attending to the real needs of your real dog on the glinting sidewalks of the Here and Now.

When what any dog needs is just for you to pay attention. We need only to *pay attention*, to vibe them with the constant assurance that there's nothing wrong. This is what our kids need too, to be told they belong here, that nothing in the world is strange, that no one is a stranger. *You belong here,* your actions need to say, as you emit the low and consistent hum that tells them you have the most extraordinary talent for keeping small beings from harm.

So very obviously I hadn't done enough to make Whistler feel calm, which is what was making him into the peculiar dog he was turning out to be. He just didn't act like what we'd expected and seemed to exhibit these Ruling Class attitudes, as if other dogs were simply not to his liking. Shouldn't a dog of mine be more laid-back and good-natured? less snobbish? more Californian?

If he was turning out to be tempermental, Jack and I told one another, this was probably because he was a purebred. Neither of us had much experience with owning expensive pets, each having grown up with more accidental animals, the ones we stumbled upon. Jack hadn't had a dog since he was little and I—who had grown up with dogs—was simply unaccustomed to the AKC rigamarole.

And dogs—all dogs—did seem to me to be different from what they once were. They now seemed almost technologically designed, they cost hundreds or even thousands of dollars, and maybe the more expensive they were, the less well put together they were, or the more easily broken? So much had changed in dogdom since my childhood at the beach in Southern California when our dogs roamed free and so did we. You never planned to get a dog in those days, your dog simply came to you, someone's having a nice dog who'd had a litter of pups and naturally this nice person would give you one.

Dog ownership then never seemed as life-and-death as it does now. My brothers and I always had dogs, plural; our dogs overlapped so if you lost one you still had another dog or two. This was before leash laws and these relaxed and easygoing beings went out the door to roam, always acting like they knew *exactly* where they were going. Our dogs were trusted to go almost anywhere without supervision, as were we. In childhood my brothers and I considered ourselves not so much our dogs' owners as their equals.

But here was Whistler, who was mindlessly afraid, just inexplicably terrified, and of such strange things. He was frightened, for instance, of all circular objects made of metal—pot lids, storm drains, hubcaps. The kids said it was like he'd been spooked by a flying saucer.

He was hyper and would rush about from room to room barking out of windows. This dog barked, in fact, at noises only he could hear, like maybe we were living in a force field, or like there was something a little *X-Files*-ish going on.

And all this stemmed, as Jack and I often told one another, from the most basic mistake we'd made, that, in getting Whistler, we hadn't simply gone out and got a mutt.

※ ※ ※

Purebred dogs were always high-strung, I'd been led to believe, and this was the logic behind our dad's going to the pound—when we seemed in need of yet another dog—to pick out the funniest-looking crossbreed. If you wanted a wonderful animal, according to my father, you'd pick the most lowly cur, that really *mongrelly* one right over there, the one made from leftover dog parts.

You got a dog, according to our dad's way of thinking, because you were in need of comic relief. My brothers and I were instructed early in our parents' theory of what lay at the heart of everything, which was profound sadness and loss. We learned by our parents' example that we needed to laugh in defiance, so we'd laugh at ourselves and at one another and especially at our dogs, who seemed to pant and smile and laugh right along with us.

We came to understand the true depths of the tragedy that lies at the heart of all existence one foggy February morning, a Wednesday, when I was nine. This was when our father, who was an architect, stood up from his drafting board and excused himself, telling his colleagues he was going out for coffee. He rolled down the sleeves on his white dress shirt, buttoned the cuffs, and pulled on his suit coat, then, instead of riding the elevator down to the Van de Camp's bakery on Wilshire Boulevard, he climbed the steps to the roof and jumped from that seven-story building into the parking lot.

Some coffee break, our mother said. *Some coffee break,* she'd always say, and the four of us laughed together at this insider's joke—you maybe had to be inside the room of our pain to really understand how funny this was to us. We needed to joke about the manner of his death because making light buffered us from continued shock. Laughter bound us to one another, as did our talent for very often saying the inappropriate thing.

It emerged as part of our creation myth that our dogs were *like my brothers and me,* essentially comic and tough and always humbled by a cosmic sense of our own foolishness. Dogs too were inappropriate, as everyone knew: In the realm of domesticated animals, it was cats and horses who'd been awarded dignity. You didn't laugh at those animals, then find them grinning back at you.

But now our half-grown purebred dog had developed what really looked like the saddest face. He'd been born on a breeder's farm way out in the country, maybe the city was too noisy for him? Maybe he was just as easily overstimulated and distracted as I was and felt himself to be just as far out to sea? Or maybe he and I were forming one of those tight and unhealthy duos where each feeds off the other's warped psychology, a theory I mentioned to Jack, one he instantly dismissed.

My husband actually dislikes the entire realm of knowledge known as "psychology," especially the notion that he or anyone he loves is possessed of one. This probably comes from Jack's growing up in a family of churchgoing Baptists. What we called *psychology* in my family of origin was more likely known to his folks as *character.* Jack left Christianity behind as a young man and is now a practicing Buddhist.

Like the Buddha, who acknowledges that there is suffering in this world, Jack understands that tragedy exists but prefers not to set up shop and dwell there, which leaves me to be the one to examine how our ornate and vivid Pasts are linked to the history of the Present, the two then working together to enact a plausible Future.

Whistler was turning out to be my best friend, my boon companion, and it was now the sadsack look of my dog's tragicomic face that filled my heart with joy, as this made him seem *like me* in my present state. He liked to sleep with his face on the tops of my bare feet as I typed, raising his head to listen as I read a passage aloud, one I thought particularly good or apt. How attentive he seemed in watching my lips, head tilted to one side, as if my dog believed me to be saying something so profound it might be worth all the effort he'd have to put forth in trying to understand it.

My dog was turning out to be a much more attentive critic than anyone else in my family, who—let's admit it—have heard most of these stories before.

I'd speak and he'd look up, all slack cheeks and droopy jowls that pulled down on this lower eyelids. He had a slightly bedraggled look, his hair as unruly as mine is and just as curly. You don't really brush or comb hair likes ours—instead, you get it wet, slop on conditioner, then run your fingers through to get the tangles out. The dog book mentioned the work involved in a springer's upkeep: "Once-a-week grooming will keep the coat shiny and beautiful, professional trimming required a couple of times a year."

It was Jack who brought home the book we'd use for research: "The English springer spaniel has a compact, well-balanced body," it said, "a wide, long head, dark eyes, and a tail that is customarily docked. Its coat is long and slightly wavy, and bushy on the ears, chest, abdomen, and legs... cheerful, affectionate, playful, and calm ..." Because Whistler was such an attentive listener, I'd go get the dog book to read these passages aloud to him. Yup, I'd tell him, It says right here, Whistler! Look, it reads *calm*. Don't you understand what it is to be *calm?*

I'd opened the book to his page and was trying to distract him, attempting to be heard over the horrible racket he was making. My dog was standing with front paws on the back of the couch, looking out the front window, growling and barking at the dark-skinned man—wearing a three-piece suit, carrying a briefcase, obviously prosperous—making his way from his own home down our street to the Cleveland Park Metro.

Jeeze, Mom, the kids had begun to say. Do you get that one of Whistler's Issues is that he's racist?

᠀ ᠀ ᠀

It was precisely because a purebred dog is designed and bred to conform to breed standards in temperment as well as looks that we'd chosen to go this way. We picked the springer because we'd been told this breed is not only merry but steady.

We needed steadiness, we knew, because so much else was in flux that year. There were too many comings and goings, all that getting on and off planes was simply unsettling, in that your body might arrive but your emotional luggage would then fail to show and you'd go off on another long crying jag.

I'd noticed how my kids suffered even going back and forth across town between their father's house and mine in our shared custody arrangement back home, in that someone's algebra book or French flashcards were always at the other parent's place. Maybe Whistler needed to be part of a tighter, more predictable nuclear family than ours?

And Whistler did need to bond with each of the four of us. This was vitally important because the family Jack and I were putting together was still a work in progress, still being constructed in mosaic, from the great shattering that took place when his previous marriage and mine had each ended in divorce.

This dog needed to bind each of us in affection, I believed, not only the four of us to the animal himself, but also my kids to this dear man who loved them but was, in fact, their stepfather and could never take the place of their own dad.

But more than anything I felt, the true use for this dog was to help me find my place in this new world, to which I'd awaken day after day—in my profound and startled estrangement—to realize again that I was in the wrong town on the wrong side of an entire enormous continent.

The spaniel belongs in the sporting group, designed specifically for hunting. The springer, specifically, had been around since the 1800s, bred to hunt waterfowl. At Westminster a dog like Whistler would be judged for his long curly ears, by the beauty and balance of his irregular markings, in either black or red, by his thin waist and full chest, both indicators of his physical stamina.

And springers have that soft mouth, which allows their lips to be elastic enough to cover their teeth as they come bounding through high grasses to bring you the duck you've shot. It's those droopy jowls and lids that give springers their characteristically downcast look.

So being true to breed standards meant a springer would bond to his owners tightly, which is why you might expect this dog to stay calmly by you when the shotgun's fired.

That this issue of tightly bonded loyalty might mean a dog would suffer when he was left behind hadn't really occurred to us. Because I work at home, we reasoned, so I'd be right there day in, day out— with my vast and all-encompassing maternity and my long and impressive resume as a dog person—to look after him.

What we hadn't accounted for was the frequency with which I now needed to get on a plane and fly three thousand miles away.

Jack and I both now traveled all the time, as it was only by moving to Washington that we found out how closely tied we were to everything and everyone in California, where I need to be every three or four weeks because I *had* to see my kids, this becoming a need so profound I felt it physically.

Jack's parents were there too, and they were getting older. Also in Berkeley was the increasingly complicated apparatus of our large and extended family, which included not only my children, but also Jack's sons by his previous marriage. Sean and Demian were grown and out on their own—Sean and Heida had recently married and were planning on starting a family. But because his boys were in their twenties did not mean they no longer needed their dad, who's close to both his sons.

As for my kids? Washington seemed such a beautifully white and marble and spacious city, as interesting as some European capital. My hope was that Noah and Eva—in visiting frequently and coming to know the town—would actively want to come East to live with us.

Eva, who was entering middle school, was likely to be pursuaded, but Noah, who'd turned sixteen and who was now rowing crew and newly equipped with a car and a girlfriend, was becoming only more resistant. My son unambivalently said he intended to stay and finish at Berkeley High.

But they still seemed like young-enough kids to me that I felt I needed to hold my daughter in my arms and to at least lay eyes on my son. I needed—for my own psychological health—to *see* my kids, needed to talk to Noah face-to-face, as a teenaged boy is not going to have any kind of reasonable conversation with his mom on the telephone, no matter how intimate they are.

So getting a puppy to help fill my cratering maternal needs was no doubt unfair to this dog. Whistler wasn't to blame for his being tense; it was no doubt my fault he was twisted and neurotic. What complete idiocy of ours to give him the job of standing in for the children I was so desperately missing.

My kids and I were all shaky and depressed. What I'd underestimated was the effect of all the physical distance that separated me from them, the weight of all that space and time—all those vast green flyover states, all those time zones—were doing to the three of us, we who'd shared an oxyginated blood supply and who are mutually entwined in an empathic connection that feels, and probably is, somewhat mystical.

This poor sad innocent dog was somehow supposed to fix this?

What usually works out best—as I've at last come to appreciate—is allowing your dog to be that one thing he's actually good at, which is, of course, being a dog.

❧ ❧ ❧

I felt the faltering of my maternal love, felt it all the time. What kind of mother was I to have allowed my kids to stay behind? Oh, sure, I understood the logical reasons and even happened to agree, knew I was honoring their wishes, knew this sacrifice of mine allowed them to stay close to their father and their friends and in a culture they understood and in a physical place where they'd always lived, and yet . . . ?

My agreeing to this arrangement meant I trusted my children enough to know they'd be all right without me. But the way I continued to feel—which was completely wrecked—had almost nothing to do with logic.

I was sad and depressed, also ashamed. I was actively embarrassed to admit that my children were living so far from me, as if this meant something awful had gone wrong, like I had some obvious genetic inadequacy, the same parental flaw that derived from crappy examples of my own mother and father. So when people I'd be getting to know asked about my kids, I'd begin long-windedly defending myself against accusations that no one, in fact, was making.

People in Washington, DC, did not happen *to care* where you'd stashed your kids. People in Washington, DC, sent off their own children to Switzerland to go to boarding school.

In truth I'd met almost no one in our neighborhood, those you might casually expect to meet by saying hello as you made your way up the alley on your way to the dog park. Our neighbornood was full of the most overt of overachievers, men and women both, all so busy out there striving and achieving that all their dark houses rattled empty during the daytime.

Oh their windows would burn brightly for a moment, just as they arrived back home, but then—and this was *offensive* to me—they'd be so work-driven and work-identified as to then need to turn in even sickeningly early so they could get up at the crack of dawn and go out and achieve some more, and so, almost immediately after dinner, the lights blinked out as our neighborhood went blank and dead again and I'd be sitting on the porch swing, my dog in my lap, asking: What kind of town is this, Whistler, in exactly which parallel universe have we landed?

&

dog boss

&

I had no friends. I had my two children, who were very far away, and this burdensome grief over all that had gone wrong in my marriage to their father, and my homesickness for the Bay Area, which had begun to present as a physical malady. And I had my writing, which was not going well, and I had this new marriage to a man with whom I was—and am—very deeply in love, but whom I needed to shield the terrifying depths of my loneliness, in that this was all bound up with anger that seemed to halo what now felt like almost a cosmic sense of loss, so soon enough I had a therapist.

So I was in treatment, and so, increasingly, was Whistler, as we'd moved to a town that prizes its experts, and whatever was going wrong with the two of us could be cured by more expensive training and maybe new and better pills.

We sent Whistler off to the countryside in Virginia for a month of sleepaway camp with Washington's foremost dog guy, famous for having trained Barbara Bush's dog Millie.

Our dog expert's name was Bob Maida. He believed in dominance training and was one of those terrifying drill sergeant types who barks orders at all the complete incompetents who show up at his place in Manassas with the dogs they've already ruined by not having the slightest idea of what they're doing.

The kids called the trainer Dog Maida. When Whistler came home a month later he could sit, stay, lie down, come, and walk at heel under voice command, but he was as frightened as ever.

He isn't better, Mom, Noah said, after taking Whistler for a walk. This dog acts like he's been in a training camp run by the Gestapo.

But Jack and I had, by now, paid so much money to this trainer that we felt we could only get out by going forward, so our dog, home from bootcamp, was still being driven by us to Manassas every Wednesday evening for skills sessions, which Bob Maida videotaped so we could take home the VHS evidence revealing everything we were still doing wrong, which was nearly everything, in that the worst dog-owning mistakes were those we came by naturally.

Number one? Jack's and my overindulgence.

Stop looking at him like that that, Bob Maida barked at us during one of these trainings.

Like what? we asked.

Like he's the Baby Jesus!

Okay, so maybe this did make a little sense, maybe we could at least dial it back and stop treating our dog like he was the Son of God, thus relieving him of at least some responsibility.

Not the Baby Jesus, we wrote, underlining *not*, then looked back up.

Jack and I were excellent students, having come to the session with the six-by-nine-inch blank book we'd bought at the Freer-Sackler gift shop that had Whistler-the-Artist's butterflies all over its blue cover so we could take notes.

Second Important Point: We both needed to stop talking to him all the time.

The voice of Bob Maida did not so much rise as it came on like a radio at full volume. THE DOG DOES NOT UNDERSTAND YOU! Bob Maida yelled at us. YOU'RE ONLY CONFUSING HIM!

Confusing him, we wrote.

When you speak to your dog, Bob Maida yelled, you are issuing commands! Use words of ONE SYLLABLE!

One syllable, we wrote.

Know what he's thinking when you talk to him all the time?

What? Jack and I said.

There they go, babbling again.

We nodded, wrote this down: Babbling again.

Is he still sleeping in his crate? the Dog Man asked.

Of course! Jack and I simultaneously lied, looking down to concentrate on writing, Continue crate training, exclamation point!

We also needed to walk him way more than we were doing, to siphon off all that barky energy of his. We needed to walk him or he'd get fat. Springers tended to get fat, we knew that, didn't we?

We nodded, we wrote the word *fat* in our journal and circled it.

So for winter, Bob Maida said, you'll be getting him a treadmill.

Treadmill, I wrote, which was when Jack reached over, took the pen from my hand, and crossed that last entry out.

ช ช ช

So much about this dog-owning thing seemed to point at every maternal inadequacy I'd ever thought I'd had, but there were also these new and ever more intricate ways to mess up.

Whistler, for instance, had dietary issues and wasn't to have even one single table scrap, as these gave him Garbage Gut, which is when your dog's bowels seem to liquify so he poops what looks like bloody coffee grounds.

Our dog was allergic to fleabites, so we needed to bathe him way more often, needing also to use medicated soap and a leave-in conditioner that we had to drive to Friendship to buy, with me muttering, *Thirty-five dollars for dog shampoo?*

In those days I was often so depressed and enervated that even reading the words *Weekly Dog Bath* written on the calendar tended to exhaust me. The mere thought of bathing this fifty-pound animal of mine, then drying him with a hair drier while he cringed against me and howled in terror, then cleaning up the horrible mess it made of the trashed and dog-hairy bathroom, made me think I'd require a good long nap before I could even *consider* it.

Jack and I had had no idea of all the money it was going to take to keep up with a purebred dog, no experience with any well-thought-out or intentional animal. Even the act of owning such a dog made us seem a little like the People Like Us to ourselves, like we'd arrived on the other side of the country and had begun to act like the PLU, that is, Upper-Crust-ish, and the direct opposites of our truer selves.

We'd gotten this particular dog by blundering along according to the theory—and my kids and I were no doubt co-authors of this theory—that Jack really needed for his first dog-owning experience since Rags to be a good one. Rags was the dog who'd been run over right before his eyes when Jack was six or seven, growing up in El Monte. Jack's losing his dog in this terrible way was the reason he'd never wanted another one.

What we needed, we all thought, was to get the right dog this time, not some accidental pooch who in all likelihood would not work out. All of us were still so traumatized by divorce and dislocation that we were sure none of us could deal with even one more traumatic loss.

It was Jack—once lured over to the side of the Dog People—who'd taken on the management of the dog-acquiring project and it was he who'd gone out to buy the book. If—that first Christmas we were in DC—you'd been standing on our snowy porch, peeking in the window, you'd have witnessed this beautiful scene: fire going, lovely curly-haired mother sitting on the couch between her two handsome children, big new dog book shared across their mutual laps, heads together, discussing the possibilities.

The book Jack chose—coffee table format, big on pictures, light on text—offered an overview of each of the breeds and included only the more basic stats: height and weight of a sire or dame, average number of pups per litter. This volume was organized alphabetically by breed within each classification—Herding, Working, Sporting, Hound, Terrier, Toy, and Non-Sporting Groups—one breed to a spread. There were always gorgeous shots of only the best-looking, most well-proportioned dogs, including a shot of a litter of the most adorable puppies.

Noah and Eva and I turned the heavy pages together, staring at the photographs, each of us weak with puppy lust.

Jack chose the springer because of these words: *merry, calm, gentle.* Early in the new year, after the kids had flown home to California, he got a tip on the breeder. In February, he and I drove deep into Maryland to Prince George's County to meet the then only-several-weeks-old pups who'd still easily fit in the palms of your hands. Then, in March—this was Easter break, the kids back with us—we all drove out to the farm to bring our puppy home.

The breeders were a young family who owned both the father and the mother. Whistler's dad was bigger, heavier, and more laid-back, which we imagined was the way our dog would likely turn out, too. Our dog, being male, would take after his father, wouldn't he? And this big guy was exactly the dog for us, good-natured, relaxed, tolerant, as his pups climbed all over him.

What we'd entirely overlooked was the sight of the mom—the family called her Speedy Gonzales, which was not her name on the AKC registry—who'd occasionally zip by in a black-and-white blur.

We picked Whistler because he romped with his littermates,

because he was a friendly, funny, happy pup, playful but not aggressive. Jack got to name our dog—the kids and I agreed—because he was still in recovery from the tragic loss of Rags. In doing his research, Jack had learned that your dog needs a two-syllable name, also one you can modulate to mean a range of things.

Jack learned that dogs listen for tonalities, for the one and two of their names. Also that you'd need variety in the ways you have of saying this name, either up into the higher, more excited range: Here, WHIST! Here, Boy! or else descending into your lower, more commanding register: WHIST-ler COME.

It was a day or two after we'd gone out into Maryland to visit the farm the first time, when we picked out our pup from the others in the litter, that our dog's name arrived as I sat working at my desk. The fax machine started working, making all these labored sounds of activation, its crinkly *whooshes* and *rat-a-tats* as it slowly disgorged the shiny paper that you then needed to rip from the rest of the roll. A fax took forever to print in those days, so you'd felt Time's Passage as you'd wait to make out the huge black Helvetica bold lettering:

James Abbott McNeill Whistler

Whistler is the painter who'd signed his name with a spotchy doodle that took the shape of a butterfly, and this, we'd decided, exactly matched the white mark on our puppy's rump.

So our pup would be named Whistler, which made me—at least privately—Whistler's Mother and in giving myself this name I felt a real lift to my spirits, as if this might take a little stab at what might become my Washington Identity.

This dog looked like a perfect dog, his shiny coat a nice balance of white and black, with that one bright white butterfly patch near the base of his tail. And he did quickly grow to be the kind of young dog people would compliment on the street. That is one good-looking animal, people said, someone stopping me every time I walked out with him. Your dog is just beautiful, people told me.

Whistler was trained to walk at heel under voice command, but I kept him on lead as we walked all over Northwest, up our alley, zigzagging onto Macomb, then to cross the whizzing thoroughfare of Thirty-fourth to get to Rosedale on Newark, or to go on to the Bishop's Garden behind the National Cathedral.

And when people spoke to me, saying *Beautiful dog,* I'd nod and murmur something in the direction of *Thank you*, never getting over the feeling that my thanking these people was something of a weird thing to do.

What do you suppose they mean by that? I'd ask Whistler as we walked away, and I did talk to my dog out loud. I did it before Bob Maida expressly ordered me to not to and I continued after I'd been told to knock it off. I spoke to my dog eye-to-eye, exactly as my own mother had always spoken to me, exactly as I too have always talked to my kids whom I never showered with babytalk.

STOP THAT! Bob Maida yelled during one of our training sessions. YOUR TALKING TO YOUR DOG IS THE REASON HE DOESN'T RESPECT YOU!

Oh so what? I said to Whistler the moment we'd escaped the Dog Boss. Respect is another of those things that's just so *vastly* overrated.

Jack spoke to our dog as well, and Whistler—at least according to my husband—spoke right back to him. They had, in fact, these wide-ranging conversations that went on and on over weeks, then months, then years, picking up exactly where they'd left off the next time they went out to walk together.

They'd need to discuss the flora and fauna of this place, to do their mutual tree census, to spot new insects, to discuss such phenomenon as the harmless clouds of cicada urine mist, also to ID every songbird that flew by. In terms of bird identification, he and Whistler—according to my husband—shared the same more than hundred-entry Life List.

Beautiful dog, someone would say as Jack and I walked out together with our young dog on some balmy summer's evening, and Jack—raised by Southern Baptists who were not socially maladapted—would nod pleasantly while I was always left to ponder all that for another little while, trying to figure it out.

What do you suppose they *mean* by that? I said to Jack. Are they praising our excellent taste in picking him, or maybe complimenting our good fortune in being able to afford a dog like this?

Jane, Jack said, it is simply just some minor pleasantry, just one of those things people like to say to one another.

Some minor pleasantry, I noted.

Having some lovely being with you does somehow render you more harmless than you ever were before, as I'd noticed when Noah was first born, seeing how this beautiful child with his mop of golden curls made the whole world shine a different light on me, as if we were both now being intensely valued for transcending what is ordinary. The universe treats the new mother and child with this glad deference, even joy, because they are so important to the shared spiritual enterprise.

With a dog or baby all kinds of people will speak to you who never would before, wanting to praise this small attractive thing of yours, pleased that you've found enough hope for the future to have gone to raid the Creature Shop.

So they'll all smile at you, admiring your stamina, your courage, your blind paticipation in what really is the most crazy act of faith.

❧   ❧   ❧

Anything small and in any way adorable also gives you and your fellow human one shared topic of innocuous conversation. Eva's pet rat

Whitney worked like this, not so much her cat Phoebe who came with us from California, but who barely makes an appearance in this story since Phoebe was a cat so strange and reclusive many people who came to our house never understood we had one.

Whitney was albino, her coat white as snow. She spent most of her two short years of life in the pocket of my daughter's jacket, Eva holding this warm bundle cupped in the bowl of her hand as my children flew back and forth across the country, her rat maybe even operating the way her bottle or snuggly blanket once did, as transitional object, and she was what Eva seemed to use to steady herself, just as Noah, for a time, took to traveling with his lacrosse stick.

People at an airport would talk to Eva about the little creature whose naked pink tail dangled from her hand or wrapped around her wrist, and it mattered not that what was said had all been said before, that, yes, she was female, named after Whitney Houston, that all the good rats are girls in that a male will simply bite you, that, yes, it was in fact entirely usual for a fifth grader to have a pet rat go everywhere with her, as all Eva's friends at Ecole Bilingue de Berkeley that year had their own pet rats crawling around somewhere in their clothing, many of them from the one same litter.

It mattered little that these same things were uttered time and time again, mattered not at all that in saying them you maybe weren't saying something much more important.

Because most people—as I was discovering—simply like saying the expected thing, which will have them restating some pleasantry, as that allows us all the superficial interaction in which there's nothing much at risk. And it's maybe true that most folks just aren't comfortable telling you what they really think, just as they don't want so much to hear about what I am *really thinking,* either.

⚥ ⚥ ⚥

Dogwalking was an integral part of the social matrix of our little piece of Upper Northwest, where I'd see all these tight clusters of dogwalking friends whenever Whistler and I went to Rosedale on Newark, or went the other way, crossing Connecticut, then following the trails down into Rock Creek Park.

And these dogs, being better adjusted and way more normal, would come racing up while mine stood trembling against my legs, whining almost inaudibly as they quickly sniffed him, immediately lost interest, raced off again, and only then did Whistler whip around, growling and snapping, at the end of his lead, like he was scaring away all these bad, bad dogs.

Sorry! I'd call out. It's him! Sorry! he just doesn't like other dogs, I said. No idea why!

Of course I should have dropped it right there but then I would have to go on—why? Because I was so monumentally lonely and this passed as quasi-human interaction, so there I'd be overhearing myself needing to add yet *another* beat to the conversation that the other people were not even having.

He just doesn't get that dogs are *his own people!* I called to those who were not listening. Which is a joke, I mentioned to Whistler, which is probably just way too fucking hard for the PLU to even get.

By which time all the PLU would have smiled their thin little patronizing smiles vaguely in our direction and returned to what they were doing, which was speaking exclusively to others who'd had the foresight to show up at the dog park with their so-much-better-in-all-ways dogs.

It was there in the dog park on Newark that my dog and I suffered the most pariah-like sense of social isolation, me standing by myself aloof and observing, reminding myself of Phoebe, who liked to shadow me as I made my way down the alleyway, her stopping when I stopped, sitting, looking immediately away to not be caught seeming to have attachment.

Here'd be all these dog owners whose dogs knew how to romp together while being casually watched over by their clutch of the usual suspects. These would be Our People, as my mother called girls and women, often blondes, often equipped with the regulation Hillary Clinton helmet head and pantsuited body of the nonfrivolously employed, each clad in the stiff demeanor that extinguishes all hint of the pliancy sex might ask of you.

Nevermind, I said aloud, these are not Our People, Whistler, and we probably don't belong here, but we have better things to do than allow our feelings to be hurt by a bunch of snobs.

⚥ ⚥ ⚥

It was easy enough for my dog to ignore the denizens of Rosedale, which is set in an exclusive enclave on one of the most Upper-Crust-ish NW streets in the most white-white and poshly privileged of the four DC quadrants.

The rest of the day, in this most diverse of American cites, was positively challenging, in that my dog, in coming upon someone wearing a turban or dressed in, say, the elaborate ceremonial costume of Sierra Leone—a not-unlikely occurrence—would just go off his nut.

Anyone who looked *different* prompted my dog to bark. He barked right *at* these people, acting almost outraged by their differentness, as if there was just something inherently *wrong* with them, and this was deeply embarrasing to all of us, as this was just *such* a racist cliché.

So I'd be going into my $175-an-hour therapist's office, with my satchels full of guilt, hearing myself start in on this, expecting the back and forth of talk therapy, though—in this new place—psychotherapy didn't exactly work like that.

Is my dog maybe reading my own unconscious xenophobia? I'd ask my doctor, who seemed to be made uneasy by the question. Dr.

Wiley preferred to allocate his time in the fifteen-minute increments it took for the quick check-in so, right after the initial pleasantries, he could begin to wrap it up. I'd be watching as he'd surruptiously glance at the watch he kept on his side table, its band neatly aligned with his prescription pad and paralleling his very nice fountain pen. I'd notice his long fingers, subtly restless and moving, itching to *at last* be writing, as his writing a prescription was the actual point of this encounter, which would have just enough of the personal in it to be excruciating and I was a little horrified to realize even my own psychiatrist had little interest in what I guessed were all my keen and original observations.

There was a saying in Washington in those days—that the town was full of powerful men and the women they married when they were young: My psychiatrist's waiting room was crammed with just such women, his practice seemingly limited to what the Helping Professionals called The Worried Well. All these sad and depleted women, who looked not troubled so much as faded, like they'd once been both beautiful and vital but now sat in a doctor's waiting room as their lights slowly dimmed, there in some drab office building near the border with Chevy Chase, women who'd gone by the rules to an even extravagant degree and were now being left behind as the new century came rolling in.

❧ ❧ ❧

My dog barked at anyone you might call marginal, those who stood together in foreign clusters, those who stood alone, those he came upon suddenly and therefore startled him, anyone who looked or seemed somehow *wrong* to him.

He barked at people waiting in line at the Uptown, the neighborhood movie theater that was just around the corner from us. He barked at the white girls in saris who sold bells and candles and cards printed with Hindu platitudes at the little incense shop right next to it. Transcendence Tranquility Bliss, Perfection of the Beyond—this shop's entire name—was run by devotees of the guru Sri Chinmoy, all young female persons, all exceedingly thin from their meditative practice of carrying on extreme forms of marathoning, running round the high school track for, say, thirty days in a row, stopping only very briefly to sleep.

Whistler barked at the weak and ill, at the old and tragic, barked at the spinning wheels of a wheelchairs, barked too at whomsoever was rolling along in one, the person Jack's mom might have called All Crippled Up.

And because of the parade of glinting wheels, Whistler barked ferociosly at the herds of Stroller People who'd be disgorged sweating from the Cleveland Park Metro, big people coming off the escalators and blinking in the sun pushing little people and none of them were folks our dog had any use for, and believe me there were *thousands* of these people who'd get off the Metro and they came all day every day all summer long on their way to the National Zoo.

My dog barked and I'd kneel to scold him, yanking his face around, holding his head in my hands, making him look directly into my eyes, as I said, What's *the matter* with you? To the people he barked at I said I'm so sorry. I said *sorry*, I said it all day, every single day.

Sorry, I'd say, my dog suffers from . . . ? and I'd lose my way as I was reaching for the word or phrase that might approximate diagnosis, roaming the neighborhood where you'd find "stranger anxiety," which—come to think of it—might be similar to what was plaguing me.

What was maybe wrong with this place was that a city might be just a little too much for the two of us, I was guessing, as he'd had been born on a farm in the country and I was from the more vacant and spacious West. Maybe this city—any actual city—would be too noisy and overstimulating for Whistler and me, maybe what my dog and I required was more quiet time out at the borders of the wild?

So I'd load Whistler into the Pathfinder, him falling instantly asleep in back—there never was a better traveler—and this was exactly as MapQuest was coming in but I wasn't yet adept. We were still using countless numbers of those huge paper folding maps with type so small I needed a magnifying glass, two or three always spread on the passenger seat as my dog and I headed out on a daytrip to discover this swamp mentioned in some guidebook. And I'd already be composing the hilarious story I'd be telling my kids that night on the phone, how according to the book you could drive to such-and-such swamp and your dog could walk with you on the boardwalk.

A swamp? I asked my children, trying to involve them in the exoticism, Can you imagine living in in a place where you can hop in the car and drive to a place so wet it needs a boardwalk?

My son and daughter, talking to me from their dad's house, would be on different extensions, Noah entirely silent, and in that tone of hers that hovers right next to offense, Eva asking, Okay, Mom, but why?

⚜ ⚜ ⚜

Whistler and I floated around the town like tourists, taking mental note of the pleasantries, but feeling profoundly uninvolved, imagining we were visiting some far-off European capital built of marble so white it seemed to gleam and levitate and which oddly lay adjacent to some swamp, me writing postcards home about this or that strange occurrence, often mentioning this exotic happening to the random individual met in a checkout line, who usually didn't find it strange at all.

And living in that uncommitted, suspended, and tentative way will actually work artistically, as real life doesn't so much intrude upon your writing, so you're strangely freed from all that normally weighs you down, which is having to pay attention to the gravity of the mundane. This is how it finally began to work for me as I became accustomed to the ungrounded feeling you might think of as Here But Not Here, and this sensation began to expand horizontally over the landscape of Time, and the hypothetical nature of my own existence now allowed me to float freely in the direction of The Past so I could begin to retrospectively forgive even some of my larger missteps—and there have been some doozies—the last being our even beginning to contemplate moving so far from home.

I walked Whistler and he was fine as long as we were alone, pacing calmly along at heel as we crossed the swamp's system of interconnecting boardwalks, dog nails seriously clicking, me scanning always ahead, alert for anyone at whom my dog might take offense, my needing to be hypervigilant as I scanned in order to give myself time to redirect and go another way.

It was quiet enough now within the electronic canopy of whirling insects and humidity, sky obliterated by the ceiling made of the arching branches of bald cypress, tupelo, maple, that I could overhear my own thinking, which is how I began to finally pull apart how our twin psychologies were working.

We'd suffered mind meld, for sure, and I'd been scaring him with my defensive nervousness, but my dog was only half right, getting that I was tense and frightened and ill at ease but not understanding that this was in reaction not to these people but to *his behavior.*

What Whistler did understand correctly was that our seeing certain people or spinning metal wheels caused us both to react, though he couldn't guess that what was actually bothering me was the hair-trigger way I was now primed to anticipate the ridiculous way he'd now start acting.

Hey, Whistler, I said to my dog aloud, maybe it's time for each of us to begin to get a grip.

§

rage

§

It's exactly as I am becoming accustomed to this Here But Not Here feeling when I understand that I will not only be able to live in this place for at least a little while but also settle down and write.

This is as Whistler and I are driving around discussing our most recent navigational discoveries, me asking, You ever notice there's no J Street in the First Alphabet? Know why? I glance in the rearview, as I used to with my kids, to check if he's paying attention. Because the letters J and I, Whistler, just happen to look *so much alike* they needed to take out J Street in order to avoid confusion, thus leaving —*just get this, Whist!*—the letter they have to spell "E.Y.E" so we won't think it's the number one!

EYE Street? I ask. Doesn't that strike you as a little creepy? But my dog says nothing, as he's out of sight in the second seat, lying down and fast asleep.

As I negotiate the grid of main thoroughfares and the intricate lacework of this city's alleyways, I am simultaneously driving up and down the ghost streets and roads of the town we'd moved from, now seeming to live in the West in a more intense way than I ever did in real life, now finding myself driving Berkeley roads through Bay Area weather during California seasons.

I'm writing a novel set in the town where I was born, where Jack and I fell in love, where my kids now are, all the way over on the other side of the country from me, a hometown that feels like a personal Mecca, the spiritual destination I physically long to reinhabit.

And I'm not even writing about the entire town of Berkeley, rather two houses on two individual streets in two different zip codes, this book concerning the love affair a woman in 94703 is having with another woman's husband who lives up the hill from her in 94708. I need to be almost magically exacting in all this caste-class business in order to precisely conjure the architecture of those rooms in which they'd secretly be meeting and all this makes me so keenly observant of detail, as you are when you've just fallen in love and the world very literally shines with a quality of light that is absolutely new to you.

I see and hear and feel everything twice and by contrast: temperature, humidity, birdsong, the hourly ringing of the Campanile, the quality of all shadows past and present falling on the sidewalk, etched crisply in the arid green-gold West but painted as loosely as watercolor here in the lusher, wetter East, where daytime slips into the blue-green haze of dusk.

Homesick, I find even the simple act of typing the names of sequential Berkeley streets—Virginia to Shattuck to Rose to Spruce—is enough to bring me back so vividly that the longing's sated even as it becomes a physical pain that throbs in the center of my palms.

Because I then will look up from my work to notice that we now live in a place so strange that I can't begin to even guess, by the color of the sky alone, what the temperature outside might be, so on any pale blue and cloudless day I might open the door expecting the Berkeley air that usually hovers around seventy and be wrong by twenty degrees in either direction. And I am always only guessing about the nature of reality, and so am always working on a long and complex equation but must proceed sketchily and in pencil, because so very, very often I am getting its most fundamental concepts wrong.

⚬ ⚬ ⚬

This was back in the Telephone Days, back when I'd sit at my desk with my dog's face resting heavily on the tops of my bare feet and might impulsively be picking up the phone to dial out. I'd call my friends, often poets or writers, knowing they'd not only be home, but also jump at the chance to answer, as those of us working at home are always just as eager to talk about how our writing is going as we are to have to keep on with the work of writing it.

This was still a year or two in advance of email, when—if you were a poet or writer working at home—you'd call your friend in his or her own strange city in some far-off state and rates were so low, after deregulation of the communications industry, you could now, surprisingly, expect to talk for a good long time.

This was back before the advent of anything like ringtones, back when you still understood, in the rooms of your mind, where the person you were calling would be physically sitting and what his phone would sound like when it rang. This was when the telephone was still that sizeable object requiring hookup and careful placement to sit weightily on a desk or tabletop, sharing the same self-importance and sense of dull necessity as a washing machine. A phone gave no hint yet of what it was to become, these small stylish personal totems into which we confide so many pieces of our most private electronic selves.

My phone friends were writers tethered in place by a handset attached by its spirally cord to a certain physical locale where this friend sat at his big desktop computer or still pounded away on a heavy manual typewriter and you could still so easily imagine the shape of your friend's hand as the phone rang and he reached out for it.

I could then readily imagine my loved ones *in place* as we spoke on the phone, which was so comforting it may be a large part of why I almost never now talk on the phone if this can be avoided. Know why? Because I really don't feel I know who you are if I can't visualize where you are, as I do depend on *context* to get my cues about the current state of your spiritual existence. What I mean to say is that *where you are* tells me so much more about *how you are* than we're often permitted to say, and we are not the same from hour to hour, day to day, in that—as we all know—people change.

People change, so I'd like to know how and what you're doing as we're talking on the phone. Are you at work? who's there with you? and what time is it in whichever time zone you're currently inhabiting and what's the weather and are you outside in it and what do you see when your raise you eyes to the horizon?

What I mean to ask is really this: What kind of conversation are we *really* going to have, by which I mean, How free is each of us to say what we *really* think?

Seeing a friend set in place in my mind was—and is—an enormous comfort to me, as so many of them ended up off here or there in all these far-flung and even unlikely venues, strewn here and there across the global landscape by someone's job or academic appointment.

Our friend Ross Feld, for instance, who was Jewish and from Brooklyn, had ended up in Cincinnati where he'd moved so his wife, Ellen, could do her medical residency. It was there they'd had their children and there she'd established her practice so it was there they were tapped down in that lapidary way that will sometimes fix your death place, as it did for Ross. So I'd be calling him in Cincinnati though that town never came to feel like the right place to me.

And it is the poet or the writer in a couple who will end up waylaid in these odd locales, as we're the ones whose job seems portable.

How long does the displaced person thing go on? I'd ask.

Worst part? he said. Four years.

Four years? I asked. Ross, I told him more than once, I don't happen to *have* four years.

❧ ❧ ❧

While Whistler was turning out to be exactly neurotic enough to be a true dog of mine, he was also enough of a purebred English springer spaniel as to cause Jack and me to feel a certain demographic dissonance. Maybe he was too classy a dog to be owned by some wild-haired writer and her more dignified husband whose youth had been spent seriously considering his family's wish that he enter the Baptist ministry.

Jack and I had started to manifest some strange PLU-type behaviors. We'd drive out into the country to investigate our acquiring A Second Home, or deep into Virginia to do dog training with Bob Maida, or to shop at some place like Orvis, such an unlikely venue, in which men and women bought lookalike leather-patched-at-the-elbow sweaters and you'd be suddenly bewitched into buying a dog bed that cost several hundred dollars.

Or we'd be going to Friendship Animal Hospital, as Friendship was one of those uniquely District institutions, like Ben's Chili Bowl or the Library of Congress, famous for its flat-out excellence. And we did always seem to be going to Friendship, as frequenting the vets' seemed to be what people like us habitually did.

Friendship was excellent, but it was also jaw-droppingly expensive. We took our dog there because everyone we knew took his or her animal there. You took your dog to Friendship because this was customary among the people we'd started to get to know, in fact,

I don't think I ever even heard the name of another vet the whole while we lived in Washington.

We took our dog there, did this unquestioningly, we also did this *all the time*, as this was where we brought him to be groomed. We paid their astonishing prices about which we then got to yelp and whine at dinner parties and we were *happy* to do all this, in that we were now being invited to dinner parties *by people we actually liked!*

Paying all this money for our dog's care and training did carry this blithe, quasi-upper-class feeling that made both Jack and me a little uneasy, the posh veterinary experience was something we were simply unused to. Go to Friendship? he and I would joke, Or take another stack of hundreds out and burn it in the street?

My parents may have taken our serial mutts to the vet, but I seriously doubt it. I think our animals went to some kind of county-run spay and neuter clinic, then got $5 rabies shots that may have actually been free. I don't remember a dog of ours *ever* getting sick and so grew up thinking dogs were like the pre-Encounter California Indians, these hardier-than-we-were souls who simply didn't have infectious diseases until the pox-faced Europeans showed up, coughing and sniveling.

But now we were living In The East in the environs of the National Cathedral and were now equipped with this Upper-Crust-ish dog, who—while we were completely in love with him—was costing us the earth. To own a dog like this you seemed to need to have way more money than we did, *more money than God,* as my la-dee-da Episcopalian grandmother used to whisper confidentially, dropping her voice to say it in order to let us know all this was *privileged* information.

⚜ ⚜ ⚜

Whistler seemed to go with the slightly false and maybe a little preposterous life were now concocting for ourselves, which derived from his having a pedigree. It was because of his AKC registry that the Springer People found us and we were now being welcomed into the springer fraternity, asked to join springer clubs, invited to springer events, encouraged to buy springer items advertised in springer magazines.

The Springer Person, we noticed, was expected to be identified as one with the breed, which is why you'd need ever more springer icons and charms, springer wallets and sweaters, neckerchiefs, needlepoint kits. You purchased these items from springer catalogs on your springer MasterCard, specifically reserved for owners of AKC English springer spaniels, that came with an excellent interest rate, for which we'd prequalified.

It was the Springer People who taught us how folks love their dogs with this ardent breed specificity. I kept going back to the dog book to read aloud to my dog what was expected of Whistler as exemplar of the English springer spaniel. I also read to him aloud about other breeds, to which he seemed to listen carefully.

By then I'd begun to notice this odd quality to the language of the book, caused by its having been written in Japanese then translated into English. The text was adequately translated into the right words and phrases but it hadn't been transposed culturally, so it still had this odd, bland Japanese politeness that seemed to honor every single breed in a measured and equal way.

It was language that emphasized the pretty, the sweet, the way-way-too adorable, and its Hello Kitty taint made the book start to seem perfumed by the delusional haze of pink time. I clearly remember that pink time from before I lost my parents, when I was still a happy little girl. Pink time is when you are still a perfect person, there's nothing wrong with you, and you still imagine your own life will turn out exactly as you'd hoped, in which you get to go wherever life takes you having miraculous adventures, getting to say and do whatever it is you want.

Know what this book is telling us? I asked my dog. That no evil lurks in the heart of a beast such as you. Know why? Because you, Whistler, are much too cute to be *an animal.*

It was maybe in that same aura of pink delusion that Jack and I moved to this town, where we sometimes felt we'd entered a pop-up storybook in which the president's motorcade would come cruising down our street, blue lights flashing, and we'd be invited to the White House, there to stand with Bill Clinton, me watching how the long fingers of the president of the United States almost completely encircled his can of Diet Coke, as Bill and Jack and our friend Bob Hass, then serving as poet laureate, were discussing the poetry of William Butler Yeats.

This is why—and, again, I'm only guessing—Jack and I, in leaving Berkeley, had begun to act less like ourselves and more like people entranced by a place, which is what happens in a fairy tale. Maybe we were under some kind of spell, which is why we'd begun to do the uncharacteristic thing, such as driving deep into the Maryland countryside to get ourselves this very expensive dog.

༄ ༄ ༄

Time, when you're on the clock with children, simply whizzes by, Time becomes Dog Years, dissolving like dew into its own pink haze, so one moment we had this tiny uncomplicated puppy, too small at first to even climb the curb, and the next we had a full-grown dog, who was both beautiful and well-behaved. To be fair, Whistler retained his Minor Psychological Quirks and Issues, but I'm not one to require a glitch-free dog.

It was almost *exactly* as we were congratulating ourselves on how well we were doing as owners of our good smart dog that we first heard about springer rage.

Springer rage? No, this just could not be. I reread every notation either Jack or I had made in the butterfly training notebook: Nope, Dog Maida had said *nothing* about springer rage.

I rechecked our Hello Kitty dog book, which—*of course!*—didn't mention it.

It was probably one of those exaggerated stories, an urban legend, based on nothing, as I told the kids, going on to read out loud: "The springer's charming facial expression makes it a popular domestic dog," then asking them, Doesn't that make it sound like a Springer will have exactly one expression? while my kids each continued to read what they were already busy reading, trying to ignore the fact that their mom was now all wrought up over her newest obsessive concern: Was there really such a literal thing as springer rage?

Springer rage? We first heard the words spoken by some new friends of ours—she was a poet, he a medical doctor—two smart and serious-minded people not given to either exaggeration or hysteria who were now worried about their own dog.

These friends got their springer pup the same spring we had, and we'd all bonded over our dogs, eventually going on Whistler's first doggy playdates, walking our dogs to all meet up at the outside tables of their son's amazing restaurant on Macomb in Cathedral Heights to have the most delicious thin-crust pizza, as they were only beginning to discover that their dog, who'd started out merry, gentle, calm, had one day dropped the Hello Kitty mask of his charming fake expression and had murderously turned on them.

As sometimes happened with this particular breed, as we were only now hearing, and this news was actually difficult to come by, also to verify, as the Information Highway was only then being built. We were truly horrified by what we were here and there sketchily picking up, that this sweet pup you'd carefully nurtured and spent a fortune training might, for genetic reasons, cause unknown, suddenly become completely and incomprehensibly psychotic. An enraged spaniel would attack without provocation, biting his owner as readily as he'd bite anyone else.

And there was no hope for springer rage, as our friends were finding out. You couldn't then send him back to the farm for retooling, as this was a form of brain seizure that could not be amended by conditioning.

Rage was the dog equivalent of the most extreme human psychosis, wires crossed, brain chemisty causing violent and toxic misfirings: There was simply nothing to be done, as with the sociopath who kills and is able to sleep peacefully in his cell, leaving the rest of us to worry if certain people are born without a soul.

If your springer behaved like this even once, he could never again be trusted. And because there was no fix, our friends' dog—almost exactly the same age as our dog—was put down.

Our friends were, of course, devastated and needed to talk about it and would stop by now and then. I understood it: They were coming by our house so they could gaze at our dog, who even resembled their dog in height and weight, but they now seemed to hold Whistler in ambivalent regard, wondering aloud how and why each of us ends up with the kind of luck we do, as there's no part of life that feels more luck dependent than that concerning an animal's misfortunes, before which we feel, and even are, so helpless.

But they were also watching him a little too carefully, I felt, looking for the first sign that our dog too might turn.

And I wanted to be a good friend to them, wanted to listen patiently, but they would be making me even more anxious than I usually am, which is sometimes even *massively anxious!* so I'd want them to just please go, so I wouldn't have to think about it, wishing us all back to the time when they still had their dog and none of us had ever heard those two terrible words, the two that now struck terror in my heart.

※ ※ ※

We appraised our dog, we looked him over clinically, we took him to the vets' to be expertly examined: Though he was still aloof with strangers and did, at times, act cross, there was no sign of rage so far.

As Whistler matured he had, in fact, calmed down. He was well-trained, obedient, and devoted, and—as soon as we stopped reacting to everyone we felt he might react to—he barked less at the random anybodys we encountered on the street. As he grew older he became more confident of us even as we—as I now imagine—were gaining confidence in ourselves.

This dog would never be easygoing but he was extremely smart. As Jack and I continued to talk to him, Whistler developed a vocabulary of more than twenty words and phrases.

He'd come, get Eva, find Daddy, woof when he heard Noah, bring his baby, fetch any ball you threw. And like something out of an Orvis ad, he'd been taught by the kids to bring the newspaper, and was as delicate with the *Washington Post* as he'd have been with the body of some dead waterfowl. He was turning out to be a good, good dog, so it was odd that—with everything going well—the Wrong Dog Dream appeared.

The Wrong Dog Dream came along just as we were learning about springer rage so the dream seemed to have ominous portent, its message seeming to be that your most cherished one—pet or husband, child or friend—might suddenly *change* into someone no longer entirely recognizable. It meant everything was unstable, that your dad could go to work some foggy Wednesday and simply never again come home and that your mom would then go crazy, and that, years later, when you believed all your thick sad past was behind you, you might one day wake up in the Wrong Town on the Wrong Side of some vast and bewildering country.

Eva said she knew she hadn't dreamed the dream, that she remembered her dreams and remembered not having that one. And it could not have been Jack, as we all agreed, in that none of us, including Jack, could remember his *ever* recounting even a single dream he'd had. It also wasn't Noah, as he himself definitively insisted.

So, as they all asserted, I may have been the one who first dreamed this dream, though others quickly came up with their own covers and renditions. The Wrong Dog Dream was adopted by the three of them, then elaborated, so they could each tell the story of the dream with complete conviction. This is what happens in any kinship system, its creation myths becoming the elastic collective phenomenon we agree to share, in which there is no one correct Truth.

Noah believed the dream was sourced in our leaving Whistler as a pup with Dog Maida, its being—in his memory—that the dog being brought out to us from the kennel at Manassas was not our dog, unlike him in every way, wasn't even a spaniel. The trainer came toward us leading a huge, tall-as-a-small-horse English mastiff, its head covered by loose and wrinkled skin so droopy as to make the dog seem to have neither face nor eyes. *Wrong dog!* the dreamer tried to say, *Wrong dog! Wrong dog!* but Bob Maida just kept advancing, bringing forth someone's genetically engineered and altogether hideous version of a canine.

Eva said the dream derived from the time she and I went to pick up our dog from grooming at Friendship, only to find he'd been accidentally shorn like a sheep, now looking so ridiculous she and I each started laughing and couldn't stop.

Stop laughing at him, the tech told us coldly. You're hurting this dog's feelings, so we'd bite our lips and cheeks and be able to stifle it for a moment, then one or the other would take another look at him and tears would spring to our eyes and we'd each be bent over laughing so hard our stomachs hurt. This whole event, the shearing and its aftermath, Eva said, caused such irreparable damage to his sense of dignity that Whistler was never the same again.

Both kids are adamant that I am the one who first dreamed it and I'm willing to believe that, though I have no memory of the original dream. Instead I watch versions of the dream as a writer watches her story unfurl, remembering each version with the same degree of familiarity. Each seems equally true, as if each is a different scene from a movie I've seen a dozen times.

Each is a dream I can fall into instantly: It's a little after three in the afternoon on a warm summer's day. I have the windows on the Pathfinder down, Tom Waits's "Bone Machine" blasting out of the pumped-up speakers. I'm making my way up Wisconsin, noticing everything, as I don't in real life but do when I'm writing. I'm as attentive to the scene as the Camera Car taking its 360 shots for Google Street View and am heading north, reminding myself to overshoot Brandywine in order to come back down the alleyway.

And now I'm on the alley and am pulling into the parking structure, which sits at ground level beneath the kennel at Friendship so you can hear the dogs barking above as you arrive. You stop the car, turn off its engine, and listen for your own dog's bark in the chorus overhead, his knowing you're here since he recognizes the sound of the Pathfinder.

I'm here! you're thinking, calling out to your dog mentally, and suddenly your heart is pained by the throb of love, your chest and stomach yawning open like a cabinet whose shelves are now exposed. This is an intense and physical sensation no different from my anticipation of the moment—hearing a car door slam or a hand on the doorknob—I'll see my husband, child, or beloved friend—after any kind of separation.

It makes no difference how long it's been—a day, a month, or year—I feel the same heart-bursting surge, a pressure so intense as to stand in the anteroom of pain, knowing I'll be seeing the one I love if I can wait just a moment longer.

⚥ ⚥ ⚥

We'd dreamed the dream that said our dog was changing but, in fact, we all were changing. It's always Dog Years when you have pets or kids, as they grow up and grow older and you can't stop the great transit of the spheres, as much as you might wish to on one of those long and perfect summer evenings that seem to want to go on forever, daylight slowly fading, but it's still so warm the kids won't get out of the pool and you're each saying to one another, Time to go in, but then no one makes a move.

We were making friends here and had constructed the rudiments of an actual life in a place that now seemed more real than fairy tale, where we'd begun to feel we might really belong.

And I was happy, joyful, to see I'd seemed to have started in the middle and yet was busy accomplishing all I'd ever wanted to do, to have these children whom I both liked and loved, and to have married into such a large and interesting family, and to be with this calm and thoughtful man, who is so gifted at happiness, who's also the best friend I have ever had, and has enabled me to do the work it takes to be a writer.

So I was happy and fulfilled, though so unused to any kind of constancy that I'd often find myself to be overwrought, tense with fear of losing this peace and balance. This fear was nebulous at first and freefloating, the occasional clutch of panic that I'd speak of glancingly in curt fifteen-minute intervals to my not-very-interested psychiatrist, guessing aloud that it derived from childhood loss and trauma, though the naming of root causes did little to make it go away.

Instead the vague fear swirled around, grew diffuse and finally coalesced and—like flour sifted over William Wegman's weimaraners—it settled on Whistler, our beautiful sad-faced dog.

It was after we'd learned about springer rage that my anxiety over losing Whistler began to build, and I now became completely spooked about boarding him at Friendship, though—as I could logically argue—this was an excellent facility where he was known, where he liked going. But now I was so terrified of the act of dropping him off that my breath became short as I started the car leaving home and my chest felt tight, and I thought I might have to go back inside to take a pill.

And it made no difference the degree to which I knew this to not be rational. I *knew* my terror was irrational but simply couldn't stop myself from playing out every tragic dog-boarding scenario, couldn't stop myself from being overwhelmed by such a pervasive sorrow at the sight of the blue woven plastic lead that the tech brought with him when he came out from the back to get my dog. They used these blue plastic leads to walk the dogs back to the enclosures: The tech would kneel beside your dog to unbuckle his collar, then stand to hand you his empty collar back, as you watch your hand reaching out to take it, tags still on and jingling, leather leash still clipped so it makes one neat unit.

And here my heart would seize, even as I was acting crisp and businesslike, winding the leash around itself to make a tidy package that'd be easy to stow, all the while studiously looking away from my dog so as to not meet his beseeching eyes.

Bob Maida had ordered us never to make a fuss over our dog in either dropping him off or getting him, so I'd barely say good-bye, would actually almost rush away, pushing out the heavy metal door at the top of the stairs leading down into the parking structure, tears in the back of my nose, racing blindly to my car, opening the door to the backseat on the passenger side, where I shoved his collar and leash that were now wound tightly together deeply into the pocket, then go around to the driver's side, climb into the seat, cross my arms on the steering wheel of the SUV, resting my head there so I could cradle it and weep.

birthday friends

Jack and I were finally making what Eva calls Birthday Friends. Your Birthday Friends are those you share intimate knowledge with, who understand not only which of your kids derives from whose previous marriage but where these kids currently are and why. Birthday Friends know your politics and religious leanings, what you do to make money, who and what you read. They don't judge you for what your parents either were or weren't. They honor you, making you feel valuable and safe.

The first was Trish Hoard, Jack's work associate. Through Trish I met her best friend Susan Bobst, and the three of us started a book club.

The first couple we got to know well were Laura Thorne, a sculptor, and Loren Jenkins, a journalist. We were set up to meet them in a blind date–ish way by our mutual friends, Jim and Kay Salter, who knew them from Aspen. Loren and Missie, as she's known to her friends, had moved to Washington at almost exactly the same time as Jack and I had moved East. Missie was famous in another lifetime as Ash Blonde in Tom Wolfe's *Radical Chic* and—like me— had come as a Trailing Spouse when Loren became head of foreign news at NPR.

We met and—as so rarely happens—all four of us liked one another immediately. We had similar interests and values and, as Westerners, shared the same somewhat skeptical view of all that Washington both is and is not. It was Loren who named the people inhabiting the world we were getting to know "Those Washington Creatures," his coinage to explain what happens when someone's soul began to melt in reaction to its proximity to power. We all watched, both fascinated and horrified, as someone's entire self seemed to grow sticky and soften, then started to gum up his or her entire spiritual works.

Because in Washington people had *real* power—as I was starting to realize—history-making power, as these people were in the mainstream media, showing up on the Eleven o'Clock News or *Nightline*, their faces and heads looking just so much more HUGE on the television screen than they did in real life. They were news anchors, reporters, writers, editors, and what they decided was worth covering had consequence for the rest of us, in that this then influenced what the rest of America thought and felt, and these decisions went on to determine who was or wasn't elected to Congress and the White House.

Missie, Loren, Jack, and I all thought being posted in the East was too great a cultural opportunity to pass up and started traveling together on weekends, going off to visit museums and to eat at amazing restaurants in Baltimore, Philadelphia, and New York—when we traveled, we always took our dogs.

In that I wasn't the only one: Jack too was now being reconfirmed in his growing neuroticism regarding putting our dog in the kennel by Jim, who always drives his corgis back and forth from the Salters' winter house in Colorado to their summer one in Sagaponack out on Long Island. Jim and Kay neither allow their dogs to fly nor be boarded, so when they're traveling outside the United States they'll hire at dogsitter to stay with them at home.

Missie, Loren, Jack, and I were soon taking our dogs with us on weekend getaways and so were forced to stay at the crummiest motels on the fraying edges of Rust Belt cities. Or, as we were quickly discovering, we could book rooms at the more upscale and grand hotels, since the rich simply *expect* that they can bring their animals with them wherever they go, which is, of course, the more humane thing for anyone to do.

Increasingly—though each privately—both Jack and I were having a harder and harder time leaving our dog behind.

So when we went to the Barnes Foundation in Philadelphia, we brought all our dogs with us and stayed at the Rittenhouse Hotel. There the bellmen, dressed in snazzy uniforms, will come up to your room in the middle of the afternoon—if you're still at the museum or have gone on to dawdle over drinks—and take your dogs for a walk around Rittenhouse Square.

Their dogs, Puccini and Sherpa, were Whistler's two best friends, the only dogs he ever really warmed to, and he fell for those dogs hard. Maybe it was those long weekends away on our adventures in which the animals were both planned for and included, or maybe he simply got used to them and accepted them as known to him. The tactic of this exuberant pair of mismatched blondes was to wear him down with their joie de vivre, ignoring his standoffishness by running circles around him until Whistler stopped being aloof and joined in. Pucci and Sherpa came into our dog's life just as he'd begun to settle in to become the calm and merry dog we'd always dreamed of.

Pucci was a purebred golden retriever, Sherpa, his hassock-shaped tagalong. Sherpa was a stray who, one summer while they were out at their place in Aspen, simply started following Pucci everywhere. He really was an Animal Volunteer, one of those pets who arrives out of nowhere and adopts you rather than the other way around. Our oldest kids, Sean and Heida, had recently acquired a young cat like this. Attaching herself not to them so much as to their old cat Molly, she was so far known only as the New Cat or the Black One.

Whistler was so gone on Pucci and Sherpa he seemed to yearn to see them. He'd learned by the sound of my voice alone when it was Missie I was talking to on the phone and how this call applied to him. He was maybe being clued in by the timing of her calls, as Missie often called to arrange a dog park date just after Jack left for work in the morning.

But Whistler's understanding of the English language, as we were beginning to notice, was uncannily precise. I'd done nothing to teach him, but in hearing the names *Pucci* and *Sherpa* in a conversation, he'd get up from wherever he was and go sit by the front door in anticipation.

Just hearing his friends' names so completely convinced him of how his day was going to go that when Missie and I were talking on a day when we weren't going to be able to get a walk in, I'd started referring to them as "The Brothers K" so as to not disappoint him.

After Whistler came to understand that his hearing the phrase *The Brothers K* in my conversation with Missie meant we would not be going out to meet his dogs, he'd heave his great dog sigh, leave the vestibule, and go lie with his heavy head on his front paws, staring at me with the most sad and disappointed eyes.

My dog was no genius, simply a good dog who was talked to all the time by everyone in our family, in defiance of the trainer's advice. He was uncannily attuned to the human voice, thus able to find what he needed in that constant bath of language.

That's okay, I'd say to him, we'll get to see your dogs later, maybe we'll go out with them tomorrow? but words like *tomorrow* or *later* would never catch on with him, as a dog's brain isn't shaped as ours and cannot contain such constructs. These are our own learned and elaborated thoughts in which we use the past to postulate about what might be enacted in some abstract future.

"Time present and time past are both . . . present in time future," as T. S. Eliot wrote, in that it's exactly there we construct our metaphoric worlds that contain both our elaborated dreams and the symbols we use to make poetry.

My dog was better at the simple nouns and verbs and could not really imagine The Future as you and I do, that place we habitually go in the theater of our minds. This is because our dogs' brains lack the enormous prefrontal lobe and its visual cortex elaborated right behind the eyes. It is there, in the loft made by our elevated foreheads, that we write our stories and plot and plan and seem able to see directly into the Hypothetical Time still to come.

The canine brain, by contrast, has evolved all those neurons and pathways that deal with the starkest sense of animal immediacy, which is why they excel in the realm of the senses. It's the dog's astonishing anchoring in the present time we observe in our animals, our seeing them hearing, tasting, smelling, *sensing* with the whole of their united beings, so much more alive in their apprehension of The Now than you or I can hope to be. We can also know that their Now is little plagued by the distractive play of imagination; rather, it's a many-layered sensory construct largely unimpinged on by language.

So, when walking with my dog, it's a scientific given that I am only fractionally as present as he is, in that he's smelling *exactly* which neighborhood dog has just peed on his peony bush, as well as the skunk who'd made its way up the alleyway at dawn five hours before. My dog witnesses the past and present folded seamlessly together into Dog Time, which might best be imagined as these moments that are pleated together in place to form a physical Present unfolding before him like a transparent accordian.

Our own sense of spatial time is usually given to either an enveloping memory of the past or to our envisioning what is yet to happen. It's in that prefrontal cathedral that you and I go to plan how our days or lives should proceed.

And it's there too we imagine the lives of our loved ones, what each of our kids might be currently doing: Noah rowing crew on Lake Merritt, Eva talking with her friends on the playground before school starts, Sean and Heida settling back into Berkeley after their being away for two years in Delaware at grad school, Demian getting ready to move with his girlfriend to Seattle.

And it's in our imaginations that we can clearly envision ourselves going to get our dog from boarding on "Monday evening," while even saying such words as *Monday* or *evening* are a couple of the zillion things that would leave him thinking: There they go, babbling again.

We are always positing this kind of metaphoric language to one another, mentioning *a summer afternoon* or *Monday evening* to one another, meaning, I'm going away but I am also coming back for you. We say "Monday evening," hoping to be understood for what it really means, which is, I will always love you, I'll never forget you, my beautiful dog, I'm carrying you with me everywhere I go.

Monday evening is any beautiful Future that lies beyond what's actually knowable, as we humans understand what our dogs cannot, that is, how helpless we all are before the mechanics of Real Time that rolls toward us, bringing with it the rude shock of what we cannot in any manner plan.

ɢ ɢ ɢ

In our book group, Susan was always stumping for us to take on the most ambitious projects, saying in a German accent, *Vee vill now read all off Thomas Mann.* All our friends, in fact, were readers and museum- and theatergoers, but for the affectionate day to day, the week-in-week-out rhythms of friendly conversation, we depended on a shared and intimate knowledge of one another's children and animals.

Trish had an ancient cat named Kate, currently costing her the earth at Friendship, but also loved our dog so much she'd stop by our house to play with him. She especially loved to rile Whistler up by playing pull-toy with him, loved his growling and his hanging on with his teeth as she'd swing him around.

You aren't supposed to play pull-toys with dogs, I mentioned halfheartedly, fully knowing this admonition would carry little weight with Trish Hoard.

Says who? she asked.

You know, I said.

Well, this pooch and I are through taking orders from the Dog Nazi, she said. He isn't the boss of us, is he, Whistler? She was always like this: Married to a DC cop, she liked to flash her Cop's Wife Badge to say she was not about to follow anyone's specious orders.

Aside from Trish and Susan, our closest friends in Washington came from the intial impulse of walking dogs together. I met Alice Powers the year Eva moved East to live with us and started sixth grade at John Eaton Elementary where, in Dr. Penny's class, she met Alice's youngest daughter, Brenna. In short order, Alice joined our book group.

Alice's dog Muffin was a Lakeland terrier cross—they'd got this dog because both Brenna and Brian, Alice's labor-lawyer husband, had the dog allergy that makes them okay with dogs whose coat is technically hair instead of fur. Alice and I agreed to meet at Rosedale, halfway between our houses, where Whistler and Muffin would not even *deign* to sniff one another, and would *of course!* never play. They wouldn't even acknowledge the other's existence but lay at our feet in the grass as she and I spoke over them, dogs elaborately arranging themselves tail to tail, staring away to look in opposite directions.

So as we bonded in our embarrassment over our dogs' snobbishness, one as bad as the other, she and I could quickly drop the dog-walking pretext, leaving them at home to meet at some great café on Wisconsin in Upper Georgetown for coffee, both just readily admitting we'd been using our dogs as props.

She and I were both teaching writing—I at George Washington University, she at Corcoran—but each was mainly at home at work on a book project. Alice is Italian American and from Brooklyn but so long in the District she'd served as my one-woman resource guide, knowing this good caterer, that wonderful dentist. I once met a tourist in a store who'd had her purse snatched and didn't know what to do, all this complicated by the fact that she spoke little English. I called Alice from the store on my cell to say the woman kept uttering the word *Bulgaria* and Alice, off the top of her head, gave me directions to the Bulgarian embassy located not four blocks from where the woman and I then stood. And when Brenna informed me I'd be needing to drive Eva to Bethesda-Chevy Chase to something called "Modell's" to buy the soccer stuff she required, I knew I could call Alice without embarrassment to ask, Okay, who or what exactly *is* a *Modell's* and how would a person go about arriving there?

One morning Alice called me to say she'd been thinking of taking Muffin into Friendship on an emergency basis.

Oh, no, I said. What's wrong with her?

I have no idea, Alice said. She doesn't look right, she just looks really flat to me.

Flat? I said, as in . . . ?

You know? Listless . . . ?

What's she doing?

Nothing, Alice said. She's sleeping. But she's been sleeping all morning. She slept most of yesterday too.

I don't know, I said. Whistler usually sleeps all morning and all afternoon, then he'll come to for a while to eat dinner, then sleep all evening and all night, as well. I think dogs can be expected to sleep an average of maybe twenty-two hours a day if there's nothing more interesting going on. How old is Muffin?

Seven, turning eight.

That's middle-aged in Dog Years. We're practically middle-aged, Alice, and think how we feel. Maybe she's just as weary as we are and needs a little lie-down.

That's what they told me at Friendship, she said.

You mean *you've already taken her to Friendship?*

Took her first thing this morning, Alice said. They checked her out, they said she was likely just having a quiet day.

I was dumbstruck, could think of nothing at all to say.

I know, I know, Alice hurried on, I'm totally ridiculous. And at Friendship they seem to be charging you extra for being ridiculous these days. That little piece of technical advice cost me almost two hundred dollars! Two hundred dollars? to tell me my dog's technically lazy?

Which is why it's to the Department of Wise-Ass Sarcasm, I said, that Friendship went to acquire its name.

ช ช ช

When Hazel was a toddler Sean and Heida brought her to visit us in the East. We gave our kids the house and took our dog and moved into a suite of hotel rooms with Demian and Suzanne, there from Seattle, everyone's trip planned so we could all be together with Eva and Noah to watch the San Francisco Giants in their first World Series in a long, long time. It was Hazel's first dress-up Halloween and she went out in our DC neighborhood, disguised as a ladybug, trick-or-treating with her usual attentive horde of seven or eight teens, as well as a huge cadre of responsible adults.

It was as we were back at the house one evening, fire going, having drinks before dinner that Hazel toddled over in the direction of Whistler and he growled at her. This was a low growl, almost imperceptible, but I was splashed with cold fear. Oh my god, I thought, would we now need to teach Hazel to be afraid of an animal in her own family? What was the matter with dogs these days, that they didn't just instinctively *get* who did and didn't belong to them and needed their protection? Dogs just weren't like that when we were kids, were they?

And it made me angry at Whistler, as if we were going retrograde, back to the bad old days where we worried obsessively about *springer rage*. We'd now *spent years* and who knew how many thousands of dollars in rehab helping him to become *such a better dog* than he might now otherwise be.

But then the thought occurred that I'd forgotten the Cocker Lady, who provided my first lession in how spaniels might be expected to be crabby around little kids. This was years before, my kids both small: I met her when she came to get the half-grown dog she'd just bought from me over the telephone, sight unseen. Noah's dad and I had given him this dog for his sixth birthday, a beautiful purebred pup who just wasn't working out for us.

When the woman called about my ad, she got the whole story as I was trying, in the spirit of full disclosure, to explain the entire situation, how this five-month-old pup, a bright honey-gold, had had just that one unfortunate minor incident, in that he'd accidentally bitten my son in the face. But there were all kinds of extenuating circumstances, I said, rushing to tell her how he'd gotten in the trash, how he'd been eating chicken bones, how our son, who was just six, had only been trying to take the bones away so Rascal wouldn't choke . . . ?

I seemed to be needing to be continually explaining all this to myself, going on to say we'd just about talked ourselves into thinking we could keep the dog—son's birthday present, our heartbreak at losing him—convincing ourselves that this was just some flukey, one-time deal when I noticed that the dog stood exactly at eye height with Eva, then a toddler.

So maybe, I told the woman, this wasn't the very best dog to have around little kids?

The woman told me she knew all about Cockers, she had two other Cockers, had always had Cockers, and that she'd be by that afternoon as soon as she could get there, she was setting out right then, stopping by the bank to get the cash, so would I please promise not to sell this dog to anybody else?

Rascal had bitten Noah in his cheek. The bite wasn't serious, but we'd taken him to the pediatrician. It was Dr. Hunter who told us that Cockers were responsible for more per capita dog-biting incidents involving children than any other breed but this isn't widely known since these are dog bites instead of maulings, as in the more serious cases involving such breeds as pits and Dobermans and Rottweilers. Still, the American Association of Pediatrics had issued a warning saying too many people were getting puppies like ours because of their HQ—that is, high cuteness factor—without learning anything about this animal's temperament.

Guilty as charged, I nodded, *Lady and the Tramp* being one of our kids' favorite movies.

So it was honestly surprising to me that the Cocker Lady showed with her own young child in tow, a boy only a year or so older Noah. When I began again to mention the reason we were giving up the dog, the Cocker Lady cut me off:

Of course he bites, she said. Cockers hate kids, everyone knows that, which is why my boy has been taught to go nowhere near my dogs.

※ ※ ※

And what's all that about, exactly, I later asked a dog trainer, referring to how some dogs simply dislike little kids? She explained it to me this way:

It isn't the little kid, per se, that the dog's reacting to, she said. Rather, he mistrusts the instablity that arises in any situation that contains both him and the small child, whose behavior cannot be predicted. The dog recognizes *brute nature* in the child, and will naturally step up to take command. *We all must settle down here!* is what his growling means to say.

What dogs do not like, she said, is any scene that's becoming unpredictable. The dog sees himself in the child, knows nature to be the wild system in which the future is a blank unknown and so is not yet written. This is why he goes on alert to bark and warn us in an earthquake or when awakened by a thunderstorm. What he's telling us is: *Nature! Nature! Nature!* No one knows what's just about to happen!

A dog understands what we tend to forget, that nature lies outside the province of human imagination and stands apart from our control. Our best witness of our own smallness in the face of mighty nature is taught to us by weather, which works in a verb-like way as process entirely predicated on instability and change. If you don't believe me, just go ahead and *try* to make the weather turn out exactly as you wished, with all that's going on with all that these days.

※ ※ ※

So the people we came to know best in Washington, DC, were just like us, all these over-the-top animal lovers, Friendship-frequenting conspicuous-pet-service-provider consumers. Truly, all our friends were exactly as indulgent as we were, traveling with their dogs whenever they could, talking about their dogs and to their dogs and assigning their dogs novel roles in their domestic comedic-dramas.

When Missie and Loren got married—this was before we knew them—it was their Two Blond Dogs, all bedecked in ribbons, with the wedding bands afixed to pouches on their collars, who led our friends down the aisle. Loren's best man for the occasion was Hunter S. Thompson and because he was Hunter S. Thompson, Loren needed a backup best man, in case Hunter S. Thompson either didn't show, or else did show up but came acting way too much like Hunter S. Thompson.

All of us were overly involved with Friendship, or so it began to seem to me, though all that veterinary fussing over Whistler was actually the kind of pet-owning behavior neither Jack nor I had even believed in before we'd move East, as it seemed to stop just short of dressing your dog in costume.

He and I did, in fact, draw the line right there, vowing to buy our dog none of those fetching outfits. Seeing dogs in Washington all smartly attired for the rain and snow in capes of tartan and those dear little lambskin fox-hunting booties you got at Orvis, each would turn to the other and bark NO!

❧

paradise library

❧

During the last years we spent living in Washington, DC, Jack and I rented a weekend place in West Virginia, about a hundred miles from the city. The trip took an easy ninety minutes door-to-door, straight up the 270 through Maryland, then along Route 70, turning south at Hancock to cross the Potomac on 522, then through the small town of Berkeley Springs—also known as Warm Springs or the Town of Bath—and out onto the country road leading to Shadow Valley Farm.

This was a converted barn sitting on the 135-acre working operation run by our landlords, the Truitts, who raised horses, grew hay, and sold cords of firewood, as they did organic vegetables to the several upscale local restaurants. The farm was in the rolling hills of West Virginia's Eastern Panhandle, a place of modest reputation and drop-dead gorgeous natural beauty. There, in a barn on a farm in Morgan County, Jack and I found a sense of peace increasingly elusive in the city.

We rented the barn after that particular morning in September forever altered the look of Washington. Jack and I went to collect Eva, now in high school, then stood with her in the gardens of the National Cathedral watching black smoke from the Pentagon billowing up a little more than three miles away under the domed silence of skies that had become a no-fly zone. We later witnessed tanks in the streets of Georgetown and encircling the Israeli embassy, the new militarism appearing instantly, and it was everywhere. We'd long thought of our National Mall as America's Lawn, going there each Fourth of July with Missie and Loren to watch fireworks. Now the entire vast expanse from the Lincoln Memorial to the Capital Dome stood cordoned off and deserted.

Washington was badly traumatized by the attacks but dealt with it in a wholly different way from New York City, spending no time at all in reflection. Instead the town *moved on,* as those in the Bush White House liked to say, getting quickly back to business. During the Bush Years of massive outlays of federal monies for which we are all still paying, the business of that town was increasingly the pursuit of two wars, the first hopeless, the second specious.

We kept the barn all the while Eva was at Wilson High, then—when she left for college—we were able to move what Jack deemed our *center of gravity* out to West Virginia, where everything is vastly cheaper. With so much physical stuff moved out into the country, we'd be able to keep a much smaller place in town. It was then Jack found the little apartment we had in the basement of the Vetters' downright grand house on Embassy Row near Dupont Circle.

Our center of gravity is overwhelmingly composed of Jack's library of nearly eight thousand volumes. The barn provided us with one large room, forty by twenty, that held much of it, the books occupying the floor-to-ceiling shelves that Tom Truitt had put along the long back wall's two-story height to house his law library. We also used freestanding bookcases to divide the space into discrete areas for dining, working, and reading. Jack's desk was down there, while I wrote in an alcove accessed by climbing the ladder to get to the loft above the bathroom.

The great Argentinian writer Jorge Luis Borges once wrote, "I've always imagined that paradise will be a kind of library." In the barn in West Virginia it seemed we were working on establishing Jack's and my personal version of heaven. Now, instead of being crowded into every conceivable space of the several regular-size houses we'd had over the years, the books were arranged so they seemed to engage in conversation.

The barn sat on the rise above Sleepy Creek, looking out over one of the farm ponds, at the west end of the woodlot a hundred yards from the barn where Katherine Truitt had her horses. Tom and Katherine lived in the farmhouse on the hill above and about three-quarters of a mile away, the perfect proximate distance affording all of us a balance between connectedness and privacy.

The Truitts soon became friends of ours and—because Tom and Katherine were willing—Eva was allowed to drive out during her senior year, bringing along her high school friends to spend weekends in the barn without us, as long as the kids conformed to the requirements of the Truitts' supervision. We believed the kids to be safe because the barn sat as within a moat on the land, right in the center of the farm surrounded by acres of fields planted in rye and timothy, almost half a mile off its little-traveled country road.

Buffered from the traffic on the road by the acres of the farm—and from so much of what seemed to be going on in The Outside World—the barn came to symbolize peace and safety to all of us. I had never before felt so entirely secure in staying by myself as I did at the barn.

It was possible to go to certain places on that land—and Whistler and I found them together and they did feel sacred—and see nothing at all made by the hand of man. My dog and I had discovered these spots by roaming down past the pond, tramping the marshy fields that lay beside the creek. But comforting too were the contrails of jets high overhead, planes streaming west or returning to Dulles, that seemed to connect us to our loved ones in the West, where our older boys were settling into their independent lives, and Noah was now in college.

Ours was a weathered building whose barn doors had been replaced by the sliding glass doors looking toward the sunset. A large and well-equipped kitchen had been added by the Truitts to the barn's north side. The kitchen windows faced west, so standing at the sink to wash dishes, I'd raise my eyes to watch the sun going down past a vast expanse of fields and hills into successive ranges of smoke blue and dusky purple mountains.

The barn was where we all finally found ourselves completely at home, the quiet there allowing time to expand so the days and weeks and months now stopped racing by. At the barn hours slowed into long and spacious days and evenings in which we read and wrote and listened to music long into nights that felt tangible and real, all profoundly comforting. I never needed to get used to that place; rather I seemed to arrive there already knowing it, just as that land too seemed to recognize me in some preternatural way.

Eva graduated from Wilson in 2003. Now with both the younger ones away at school and the two older boys settled and well employed, all our kids seemed to be exhibiting the patterns that said what kind of citizens they would become. Sean and Heida had had Hazel, now turning three, and were planning for another baby. Out in Seattle, Demian and Suzanne were now engaged to be married.

It was during this quietly raptuous time when everything seemed in balance that Jack sent me this quote of Alberto Savinio's, the message appearing as a subjectless email:

> Once children leave, the union between husband and wife is purified of its practical reasons [and] retires into its own pure reasons, entering into *the condition of poetry.*

> *Italics mine,* Jack had added.

Now, on a day-to-day basis—either at the barn or back in the city with him—it was just the two of us enjoying the childless honeymoon we really never had, together with what seemed like truly the most wonderful dog, as Whistler—and no one was more surprised than I—had evolved to become the best of dog companions. He and I now hiked together in Great Cacapon State Park or got up in the earliest light to walk the length of the creek up to the pontoon bridge marking the edge of the Truitts' property. I was calmer than ever before, feeling as peaceful and fulfilled as when I'd been pregnant with my kids. Maybe now, I thought, I might be able to lower my anxious guard.

I'd stopped obsessing over my own impotence in regard to world affairs, though I had the practice of lighting a candle every day on Jack's Buddhist altar to remember those involved in wars everywhere being fought by less fortunate mothers' children. Political Washington seemed increasingly far away.

I was no longer holding my breath, lurching from one parental crisis to the next, and so became intensely observant of that lush green place, attentive too to what I was reading and writing in the quiet in which the phone rarely rang and web access was dial-up and slow and intermittent.

I could now become lost in my writing, then go out to hike long miles with my dog, feeling an expansive pulse of well-being filling my heart and lungs, to catch myself saying aloud: Whistler, will you just *look* at the two of us? we look so well-adjusted! and guardedly thinking to myself: *This is happiness.*

It was such a profound and physical pleasure to feel safe, to not be stressed and doing the work of mothering, which demands the attentive pressured logic of constant problem solving, to feel little more than the pleasure of being mindlessly alive.

Because this is the truest lesson our animals have to teach us: We can lose ourselves in the physical moment by following along with them into the purity of sensual awareness. I envied my dog a reality that seemed so much more various and interesting than my own, him being not word-ridden or haunted by a dark, unending past or shadowed by my fearful anticipation of the future. If my dog seemed to live so much more intensely than I did, it was because his world was so little caught up in the imaginary.

Many days we spoke to no one aside from Jack, who'd call from the city first thing, again at dinnertime, then again to say good night. Whistler and I would fall asleep with the glass doors open so we could hear the creek rushing over boulders to sleep deeply, dreaming of nothing. We'd then arise at dawn to work, taking a moment first to sit on the barn's steps with a good cup of coffee—we had Peet's shipped from Berkeley the whole while we were living in the East. My dog and I sat together watching a green world coming alive, easing into day brought by all that magnificent West Virginia light.

As my anxiety lifted, I felt the physical weight of what has been an almost perennial sadness begin to fall away from me. This sorrow—with me since I was orphaned—registers as blinding, bewildering anger or the vague and unlocalized pain of impacted grief.

But now I felt so well, so light, so at home in my physical body. This was the same bouyant sensation I'd felt when Jack and I first fell in love, when we seemed to have been delivered into the realm of *possibility,* a limitless world where everything throbbed with meaning, as it does in poetry.

❧ ❧ ❧

An easy drive up from the city, Berkeley Springs has been famous for its baths since Indian guides led the first Europeans here, an initial surveying party that included the then seventeen-year-old George Washington in his older brother's charge. The spas are fed by natural springs constant at 73.4 degrees and they've long been the town's main industry, together with glass manufacturing from the large deposits of silica in the river and streambeds. Those early glass factories supplied our entreprenurial first president with windowpanes for the buildings of the capital city that would be named for him.

Turning left onto Spriggs Road, left again over the creek on the one-lane bridge, then left at the row of mailboxes on posts, a mile or so down the gravel lane to park at the fire ring in front of our barn.

Whistler leaps from the Pathfinder, leads me around to the kitchen where I let us in, a door that won't be locked again until we leave to go back to the city. Whistler sniffs to discover which creatures have visited during our absence, one being Moochie, the Truitts' hand—he's come by to cut and stack more firewood for us. He and Tom log the woodlot, its hardwood cut into stove-size lengths with a portable saw run by gas generator. Moochie, Tom, and Katherine all waved at Whistler and me as we drove in, all three still out on riding mowers in the fields. Late afternoon, air alive with the bright smell of grass, flecks of silver flickering in the fading sunlight, air humming with the sounds of their industry coming at us from three different directions.

I make dinner, we eat, and though the day's warmth is still with us a chill has crept in, so I kneel to build a fire in the stove we use to heat the barn's main room. The sliding glass doors are standing open, screen door pulled against the whirr of insects. I make a pot of tea, then sit by the fire to read, Whistler lying beside me, as peaceful a dog as I've ever known.

All along the long wall the shelves are organized according to Jack's own personal Dewey decimal system, so if I need something when he's not here I must call to ask him, discovering again his astonishing memory for the placement of thousands of volumes. His sense of location is so concrete that when I phone him to ask, Louise Gluck, *Meadowlands?* he'll immediately respond, hardcover, gold spine, six or seven in from the right, I'm guessing, eye height on the poetry shelves as you face that wall when you're standing at the head of the dining table.

I've told Jack time and again that he must write of his life in books, but he thinks his has been an ordinary one, having no appreciation for what a memory palace his library is. I am going to lead him through the telling of these books' stories, where they fit and how he came by them, how it's all connected. We'll call it *The Paradise Library,* which has been his life's work, begun when he started his first bookstore at age eighteen. He's collected them for himself, for us, for posterity, so every great book is here, enough for our lifetimes and those of our children's children's children, and it is only Jack who can explain how all its systems of knowledge work together.

I write in the loft up a ladder where my dog can't come, but he's lying right below me, settled in, one white paw delicately placed atop the other, gazing out the screen door as he listens to the night. Whistler: city dog of noble sporting breed, who's accommodated so easily to this place because—I'm figuring—he was born on a family farm with similar sounds and feel and rhythms. He now hardly ever barks though he does seem to hear and see and even understand everything.

The great peace of this place, its creek and ponds, fields full of night sounds, horses neighing in their barn less than a quarter mile's distance, night so alive it's almost noisy with electric whirl of cicadas, night birds cawing, far-off howl of coyote.

After working for an hour or so I climb back down the ladder, put on the tea water, turn off the two tall Library of Congress lamps acquired for the pure colorlessness of their bath of saturating light, put another log on the fire, then sit with my dog waiting for the kettle, watching as the stars dim in the spreading moonrise, lopsided orb tonight just three days shy of full.

❧ ❧ ❧

The barn may have felt like home to me because it was so like the wild place where I first swam into consciousness, that is, my first knowledge of myself as a living being of this world. My earliest memories are of the mountains above Santa Cruz where my parents had a vacation cabin. The year I was three our mom, then pregnant with our little brother, stayed in Boulder Creek year-round, while our dad worked at a small architectural firm in San Francisco in which he was partner, driving back and forth on weekends.

We'd hear him late on Friday after my older brother and I were already in bed; we'd get up to see if he'd brought us something. Our dad, the extravagant giver of gifts, often came in overburdened with bags from Gump's and Magnin's, skin of his face cold, fabric of his suit coat smelling of pencil shavings and tangerines, as he picked me up to kiss me.

Hank and I were free to play on the soft floor of the forest of coastal redwoods and oaks. We had the big black Lab named Doctor Ross our dad got Hank the week after I was born, named for the dog food commercial that went, *Doctor Ross dog food is doggone good, Woof!* Doc went with us everywhere.

So the first world I can remember was this seamless place in which my brother and I, together with our dog, were free to play outside. The cabin's living rooms were up a flight of outside steps over a storage room and garage. Our mom put her easel up out on the deck so she could keep an eye on us as she painted. I remember the smell of the thick carpet of the forest floor, the crisp beams of sunlight that streamed down as heavily through the dark canopy as something possessing physical weight. The redwoods were huge and ancient, like ancestral presences that crowded in, lacy oaks growing only within the sunnier clearings.

I came alive in that place, as if born into nature's majesty. The parents I first knew were like characters in *A Midsummer Night's Dream*, that is, almost regal and even magical, our beautiful mom, painting in oils, smelling of turp and linseed oil, her golden-brown hair stuck by brushes and caught in a topknot at the back of her head, our father too so tall and good-looking and happy.

When you left the cabin's clearing, someone noticed, if you wandered too far up the road, someone kind would help you home. The Second World War was over, peace was the state in which we now existed, our nation seemed invincible and childhood like another, more magical country.

⚮ ⚮ ⚮

I felt so safe and calm at the barn I'd begun staying there for longer stretches of time, Jack going back and forth to his offices in town but always coming out to spend weekends with Whistler and me. I'd published the novel set in Berkeley to critical successs, was now working on a large and difficult project for which I hadn't yet found a shape. This work was dark and it frightened me.

I was afraid of what I was working on but not of the place I'd come to do this work. Being alone at the barn in West Virginia with my dog was, in fact, deeply comforting, like I was at last beginning to understand the many ways in which being alone has nothing to do with loneliness.

So our leaving Whistler in boarding in West Virginia when we traveled to California was something I'd come up with. I was the one who thought it up, who stumped for it, arguing against my having to take the time to drive him all the way back to the District so we could leave him at Friendship.

It took hours, days, entire *weeks* to persuade Jack, telling him over and over how all this only made logical sense, asking him why couldn't we behave—for once—in a way that was both practical and modest. Did we *really* need to trundle our dog all the way back to the city when he could so easily stay out here in the country where he so obviously felt at peace? Why couldn't we use the kennel right down the road from us?

But Jack had years of trusting Friendship, where we'd paid them so much money the vets seemed to have something like a proprietary interest in our dog, their never letting us go without our needing to schedule a follow-up.

See, I said. This is actually twisted, it's like he's Friendship's as much as he is ours. I feel like we're only borrowing him half the time, like he's the library book they think we don't really take very good care of.

Didn't Jack see that Whistler was so much calmer out here than he'd ever been in the city? that he had finally become the settled-down dog we'd always hoped for? This was because country dogs were simply more laid-back, I said. Country dogs haven't gotten lost in status confusion, country dogs still knew they were animals, because that's how they'd been treated by country people. Sure, maybe these folks were less sentimental about their pets than we were, but wasn't this a good thing? wasn't it more realistic? wasn't the whole Friendship thing less like a trip to the vets' than a lifestyle experience?

Jack's grandmother was a country person, as I reminded him, and he'd loved his Gramma Crist, who was no-nonsense and unpretentious. There was no one more kindhearted, but she'd once drowned a sack of day-old kittens that Jack's and Vic's cat had gaven birth to, doing this without their knowledge to save them the hard choice, as she believed them to be too young and already massively over-burdened with Sean, then a newborn, to take care of even one more tiny dependent thing.

Jack's Gramma Crist had lived with his family as he was growing up and it was she who'd loved him fiercely, unreservedly. She was a steady presence, instuctive and bolstering. She'd always ironed his clothes for him, then, when he was a young teenager, she'd taught him how to press his own shirts and khakis just as expertly.

Gramma Crist ate leftover cornbread sopped in buttermilk for breakfast, she grew red geraniums in coffee cans, kept chickens in a coop in the backyard in El Monte, raising them for both meat and eggs, and would kill a hen herself to roast after church on Sunday. His Gramma Crist, as I told Jack, would completely get the kennel woman.

The kennel was on 522 right at the end of our road, just at the left turn onto Spriggs Road. I'd stopped in to visit with her and to look the place over: It was clean, heated, it looked well run. True, it wasn't Friendship, but *sheesh,* Jack, I said, maybe this dog needs to not always go to the Ritz-Carlton of pet hotels?

But Jack trusted Friendship, he said. At Friendship they knew our dog, Whistler was used to the people there.

I went on and on, relentlessly: What if this is us still secretly treating him like the Baby Jesus? I asked. What if we're trying to respoil him after he's gotten better? Why couldn't we all, for once, settle for the solution that wasn't out-and-out extravagance?

The kennel down the road was my idea, I found it, I was the one to take him. The boarding area was a concrete block building set out at the back edge of her property, room for six dogs, only half full the day I brought him in. She was all right, I told Jack, maybe a little cool, but this was an affect common among the hardworking women of that rural town who'd seen their lives scrubbed of most illusions.

Single mom, smoker, no stranger to the tanning beds, blonde of the yellow-ochre variety that had me swear off ever dying my own hair again, clenched mouth that came from holding the world together with the thousand-pound pressure of the muscles of your jaw, a look I knew well from my own face in the mirror in those years of raising teenagers.

Your boys help out? I asked, readying to leave. I was being careful not to make a fuss in saying good-bye to my dog, so I patted him once, then handed her his lead.

Yeah, she said, when they feel like it. Then she added over her shoulder as she led Whistler away, But what can you expect from boys?

This was March. Jack and I were flying to California for an eight-day business trip that had been planned to coincide with our grand-daughter Hazel's third birthday.

We'd come on Monday; by the following Saturday, spring had arrived with full-on pageantry and we'd assembled in the backyard of Sean and Heida's house for Hazel's party in sunlit air so clear and so radiant that every shadow looked etched in precision. Tulips up, magnolias out, citrus fragrant on the delicate breeze. On a day like this the gauze simply lifts away, you feel like you can really see and hear and finally understand what is and is not important.

And I recognized again what I've always known: that it takes a certain cultural weather to raise a happy child, that Berkeley goes a long way to providing this. If you can get past the tinge of sanctimony, this town can seem like such an all-encompassing, pre-forgiven, and forgiving place, where your world is full of smart, kind, lovely people, or so my parents thought, and why I was born here and brought home to their little house at 1632 McGee, just four blocks from Sean and Heida's on Bonita. This too is what Jack and I understood in choosing to raise our children in Berkeley separately, then together.

It was such a warm and glorious afternoon that Hazel and her friends had all taken off their clothes in order to play T-ball. They'd taken *all* their clothes off, having evidently settled on what they call *nakedy* as their team uniform.

On a day like Hazel's third birthday, it was so easy to remember that it's our children and our dogs who know the truths of existence, that each of us is probably born knowing all we need to know, if only we could remember what that is. Dogs and little kids just intuitively get how we use words to name ourselves away from reality and the further we move from the basics the more confused we become. It's in losing touch with our bodies that we are doomed to feel alive only behind our eyes, as we wander off into the wilderness of language.

If the work of childhood is play, these five little girls were taking the job of naked T-ball as seriously as the most dedicated CEO. Photos from this party show me watching them as I sit on the edge of the deck with Jack's former wife. I have a quizzical look on my face. I can remember exactly why.

Victoria, voice urgent, turns to me and says: You have to *make Jack* move back home. You have to do it soon. Just look at this. Look at everything you're missing . . . ?

Me, nodding, making my sounds of mild assent, going *I know, I am, we will*, even as I'm silently thinking, No one *makes Jack* do much of anything, Vic. Also, how is it that we *aren't* actually missing this? in that we're sitting here, aren't we?

The name of the relationship Vic and I share is one we've borrowed from Spanish. She and I are *commadres,* meaning, we share grandchildren. All Hazel's many grandparents, taken together, are all *compadres*, which is shortened to *los compas* in affection.

And we *are* affectionate, in that it has become the style of the kinship system that's evolved to make it a point to celebrate holidays and birthdays together. We've now been at this long enough to become good at it. We call it The One Cake Rule, meaning, You get one birthday cake and everyone's invited to have a piece of it. And these are often big cakes, as the welcomes extended in all directions outward to all involved in the lives of any of our children—step or full or half—so a party like this might easily have twenty people who'd count themselves as close relations.

⚼ ⚼ ⚼

Hazel's party was on Saturday. On Sunday Heida and I went out to lunch together at a bistro on Shattuck Avenue. It was early the following morning, that Monday, as Jack and I stood in the foyer of the San Francisco condo. Mary Turnbull, the widow of Jack's partner Bill Turnbull, had lent us her place. It was with Bill Turnbull that Jack founded North Point Press. I met Jack when he bought my first book for North Point.

Jack and I were eager to get home and were all set to leave Mary's for SFO. Her condo was at Opera Plaza in the Civic Center where the traffic—even this early in the morning—was already crazy. We'd asked the cabbie to call us when he was five minutes away so we could start down to the lobby. We had our rolling bags crowded into the vestibule ready to hop on the elevator. So when Jack's cell phone rang, we believed it was our taxi.

Instead it was Trish in Washington, calling to say the woman from the kennel just phoned her at the office to say Whistler was dead, that he'd inexplicably died overnight in her kennel. He had not been sick, Trish related, so the woman hadn't taken him to the vet. She'd just gone out that morning and found his body.

Jack called the woman, whose name I cannot remember. He said she'd sounded curt, defensive. These things happen, she said. Dogs die, all day, every day.

No, they don't, he said. Dogs do not die without cause.

Maybe his heart gave out.

He was six years old, Jack told her. His heart did not give out. Our dog was completely healthy when we left him.

She would not apologize, wouldn't soften or commiserate. We were completely bewildered, in physical shock. I started shivering. It was six thirty in the morning in California, we were disoriented. Our cab arrived, we somehow got our bags downstairs to the curb.

As we rode south along the freeway, Jack called Moochie and asked him to pick Whistler up from the kennel and to take him to the local vet to see if they could figure out what happened.

We were too stunned at first to cry. We didn't cry until we got to the airport, had gone through security and were sitting at the gate.

We kept turning to one another to ask, Is this really happening? None of it makes any real sense, we each said. He was completely healthy, we told one another. Each of us said the same things over and over again.

Maybe he was poisoned, I said.

He wasn't poisoned, Jack said. The other dogs would have died as well.

I was now sizzling with anger at the kennel woman for being so unfeeling. Anger—and anger only—was giving me the sense of purpose and direction I needed to get on that plane and make it back across the country.

Being angry was also the only way I could stop feeling what I was feeling, which was bewildered, brokenhearted, all but staggered by my own cataclysmic mix of grief and guilt.

I got up and went to the bathroom and cried as I washed my face, talking aloud to myself. You did this, I said to the stunned blank face in the mirror: You made this choice and what was that all about, really? that Friendship was too good for your dog? so you needed to put him somewhere that just invited tragedy?

The entire enterprise of flying back across the country with our dog lying mysteriously dead was so dreamlike and surreal that it's all but lost to me. Had we been drinkers we could have gotten drunk. Had we gotten drunk we might have gotten really good and drunk on that plane, so drunk we wouldn't have been able to drive the hour and a half between the airport and Berkeley Springs and so would have needed to check into an airport hotel at Dulles to sleep it off. Had we been drinkers we could have then sat in the hotel bar, then staggered up to our room and made soppy, weeping love, then fallen into a drunken sleep and not have had to deal with it. Had we fallen asleep we might have been able to dream a better dream, the Wrong Dog one in which—for what is only one long and sickening instant—you're panicked to think you've lost your dog but then awaken to find him lying right there at the foot of your bed so you can murmur softly, reach out, pat him, then curl again around your husband, as you all fall back asleep.

Sober, dry-eyed, we studied the problem and found no solution. None of it made sense: The woman was cold but she wasn't crazy and would never have harmed our dog on purpose. We could not fathom what had gone wrong. It simply did not happen, did it, that happy, healthy, well-cared for dogs died in boarding for no apparent reason?

Maybe he'd pined away, maybe he'd died of missing us, maybe dogs who've misplaced their people lose their will to live, maybe he died of plain confusion in being stashed away in some strange place or died of sorrow because we'd now been gone for *eight long days?*

And we only just missed him! I said my voice rising. Had he lived only one more day, twelve or fifteen hours, max, we'd be pulling up her driveway and going in to get him. She'd told me we could pick him up whenever we got in, no matter how late it was. I heard myself and knew I needed to stop speaking, as the sound of my wailing voice was troubling both of us.

Had he lived, I thought, our dog would have known we were almost there because of that witchy thing dogs have that picks up your time and location. Their temporal perceptions are mysterious to us but experiments demonstrate that when an owner's arrival is imminent his dog will go stand at the door on alert. *Had he lived*, I thought, he'd have picked us up on his witchy radar, he'd have had us pinging off the cell tower the moment we'd entered his area. I kept thinking it over and over again:

Had he lived.

         ✄   ✄   ✄

We somehow got to Dulles, somehow managed to collect our bags, somehow found our car, somehow drove out of the airport away from the District and toward West Virginia. Word had been spreading throughout the elaborated family tree, Vic's calling to say how sorry she was and asking us what happened. Each of the kids had left similar messages, Eva calling either Jack's phone or mine six or seven times.

As we made our way south, Jack and I began to talk about what each of us felt in leaving our dog, how scared each had been and how we'd never spoken of it in order to shield the other from what seemed like neurotic worry.

Jack said he'd long been frightened this might happen, worrying constantly when our dog wasn't with us, becoming more anxious as the years went by so now for days before we needed to drop him off, Jack would be thinking we were just about to lose him, a worry that never eased up until we had Whistler back with us.

And for the first time I confided in my husband about my obsessive terror over the sight of the tech coming toward me holding the blue-plastic lead and then handing me the weight of our dog's empty collar and tags. I told Jack how I'd started to imagine the Wrong Dog Dream to be a warning or premonition. The dream was set at Friendship, wasn't it? So Friendship had become the drop zone of my anxieties in the cascading logic of all this illogic.

The Wrong Dog Dream being the real reason I didn't want to leave him there because I was now clinging to all kinds of magical beliefs, that Whistler would be weirdly safer in the kennel at the end of our road. The kennel woman's place seemed like the direct opposite of Friendship, so I'd decided it would be where my bad luck with loved ones wouldn't know to look for him.

The kennel woman too had left a message on my phone when we were in the air. I scanned it for any sign of warmth or humanity, anything, that she might be at least clued in to the enormity of what had just happened.

Nope. I played the message aloud for Jack: kennel woman, blasé, all business, wanting us to arrange to get his things—leftover bag of kibble, leather lead, collar with his tags, asking us to stop by to pick up the exact shape of the same weight of grief I'd spent years dreading.

ᴥ ᴥ ᴥ

Losing Whistler was the most irrevocably terrible thing that had happened to Jack and me as a couple, and we didn't know how to behave, let alone understand how we'd be able to cope.

We were so exhausted we couldn't move. Jack had originally planned to drive to the city to go to the offices the day after we got back but now he wasn't up for it, so stayed out with me in West Virginia. We'd gone to bed Monday night and now stayed in bed all day Tuesday, lying there like we were sick, each pinned to the sheets by the weight of our monumental sorrow, each privately thinking about our sweet black and white dog, the pup with the butterfly spot on his rump, that he hadn't lived long enough to have just died as he had, alone and in boarding! alone and for no good reason! died alone in some strange kennel run by a cold and unfeeling woman!

And it wasn't Friendship, I wailed aloud, *but some strange place that contained no memory of our ever coming back for him!*

What I didn't say, because it troubled Jack when I did: *And it was all my fault!*

I kept coming back to the way the kennel woman's face set when she spoke of her sons, speaking of her boys as worthless and how I'd recognized the coldness in her. I should have changed my mind right then, knowing that a person who didn't like her own kids would create a place that functioned on that same efficient lack of kindness. I'd known what her soul contained and had left my dog in her care anyway. This meant I had failed again.

Moochie told us he'd heard our dog barking his sharp distinctive bark each time he'd driven on Spriggs Road in his truck going to and from the farm.

Of course he barked, I thought. Whistler was out there all alone, asking for recognition.

⚮   ⚮   ⚮

The local vet was a homeopath, and it was she who helped us arrange to have our dog's body cremated. She hadn't done a full autopsy but was certain Whistler died of a condition called bloat, which sometimes happens spontaneously as a reaction to the stress of kenneling. It's common, she said, in dogs with large chests and narrow waists, such as poodles, borzois, Labs, English springer spaniels.

What may have happened, she told us, was that he'd gulped air as he was barking. Or he may have stopped eating, then wolfed food and gulped water in deadly combination when physiological need set in.

She was sorry, she added, so very very sorry, and she held us as Jack and I stood in her office with our arms around each other and fully broke down and sobbed.

⚮   ⚮   ⚮

I would call the kennel woman without even knowing I was about to do it. I'd simply find myself standing at the wall phone in the kitchen, dialing the number I'd now memorized.

Bloat, I say. He died of bloat.

Never heard of it, she says.

Nor had I, I say, but guess what? I'm not the one who's running a kennel.

She's silent. I keep giving her the chance, an opening, all I want is for her to say one human thing.

It's caused by barking, I go on.

Dogs bark, she says. This news to you?

Not like that, I say. He was barking so loudly Moochie could hear it from Spriggs Road.

I wait, then add: If Moochie could hear him, so could you.

I wade into her silence, waiting, waiting, and she finally speaks: Okay, she says, go ahead, sue me, get it over with. You people come up here to the country with your city money and your fancy pets and act like you own the place. You want my kennel? Great, go ahead, take me to court, you'll win, take my house, my business, put me and my kids out on the street.

That had not occurred to us, I tell her stiffly.

Why not? she says. Your husband's a lawyer.

He isn't either.

Well, he drives a lawyer's car.

Know what? I explode. *You're an asshole!* and I slam the phone down into its cradle. There was no hope for this, it made no sense to try to talk to someone so belligerantly ignorant, so why did I keep doing it?

❧ ❧ ❧

We'd traveled all day Monday getting home, went to bed where we stayed all of Tuesday. Time went vague on us. At some point the kennel woman shopped at Walgreens, buying a huge white sympathy card that she had her boys drop in our box. It was printed in silver, dusted with sparkles, some grandeloquent Christian message done in flowery script.

Sorry for your loss, she wrote, not bothering to sign the card. Inside the envelope she'd stuck the bill, charging us for boarding Whistler for seven days, discounting the charges for Day Eight because our dog was dead by then.

I was sizzlingly, explosively, sickeningly angry while Jack had gone calm and still. We had little to say to one another, each too upset to talk, too miserable to either stay awake or fall completely to sleep.

Eva was calling a couple times each day to check in.

We're better, I said.

No you aren't, she said, adding that she was becoming seriously concerned.

Don't be, I said, we're basically fine . . .

FINE? FINE? she said, you call this *FINE*, Mom? she asked. You sound worse than you did yesterday. Put Jack on.

Jack took the phone from me, then moved off to stare out the window as he talked quietly to Eva for a long long time.

Later that afternoon Eva called again, now threatening to drive the ten hours down from college if we couldn't get it together to go grocery shopping. Because we'd been away there was no food in the fridge, but this was immaterial since we were much too distraught to eat.

We'll shop tomorrow, I told her.

No you won't, Eva said. I happen *to know you,* Mom. You have no intention of shopping tomorrow. I handed the phone to Jack for him to handle, he took it and spoke to her calmly and soothingly. Later that afternoon, he got up, went to the bathroom to shower and shave, then came to stand by the bed next to me, fragrant with soap.

You need to get dressed, he told me.

She is our *minor daughter,* I said, and not someone we're required to take orders from.

But she happens to be right. We need to get up and go out to get something to eat.

No, we don't, I said. I couldn't possibly.

You really do need to change clothes.

I looked down to remind myself what I had on, one of his too-big tee shirts and the same underthings I'd traveled in.

You'll feel better when you're vertical, he said. You need to run your fingers through your hair, splash some water in your face. I'll take you to the Warm Springs Café for dinner, okay?

No, it is not okay, I wanted to scream. My dog's dead and the two of you won't stop badgering me.

We were not better, as Eva had so easily discerned, and were, in fact, so much worse. Marriages did not survive these traumas, I could feel all affection slowly leeching from ours. Soon Jack would begin to fully apprehend the horror of what I'd done and he'd commence to blame me. Why shouldn't he, as I was the one responsible?

I kept revisiting how the kennel woman had been already known to me, how I'd understood her on some deep level, known she wasn't kind, yet had left our dog with her anyway.

There being no hope, our intimacy would now erode. Jack was already looking at me sternly, his most cold and discerning expression, already judging me and finding me unsatisfactory. I gathered up my things and went to the bathroom to get away from him, pulled on jeans, another tee shirt, scuffed sockless into a pair of battered running shoes, then turned to see myself in the mirror, peering out through painfully swollen eyes at hair so badly tangled it had started to twist into ad hoc dreads.

My hair looked nearly as bad as after our father died and we were left in the care of our mom. My brothers and I watched as she descended into madness, this taking six or seven months. We stayed with her until the day we were unceremoniously scooped up and delivered to the house of our aunt and uncle and she went to the mental hospital, where she stayed for the next ten years. By then my hair was a matted ruin, no hope for it at all, nothing to be done except what my aunt then did, take me to the barber who used electric clippers to shear it off short as a boy's.

⚥ ⚥ ⚥

We drove to the café, which Jack liked while I did not. I liked the older lady and her two more our-aged daughters, each kind and humorous and friendly when we'd been in before. What I didn't like was the terrible food, chicken-fried chicken, chicken-fried steak, chicken-fried everything. They call it "homestyle" but in whose version of "home," I wondered, must they deep-fry every blessed thing?

A vegetarian would die in Berkeley Springs, which made no sense since this was farm country where these same people had been raising fruits and vegetables for 350 years. Now there was virtually nothing to eat aside from the grim product lines of industrial farming, overcooked green beans floated with specks of greasy ham, Miracle Whip slathered straight from the jar onto the commercial white bread they used for sandwiches, all this mess bought by the hand-truckload at the Walmart down 522, everything brought to you by those friendly folks at Monsanto.

The younger prettier daughter served, her sister helping their mother in the kitchen, all of them bantering humorously, the two in the back peeking through the pass-through to say hello to the locals as they stopped in.

Jack liked this place, I knew, because it reminded him of his

Gramma Crist—she was simply *so unlike* the women in my family. My grandmothers learned languages, they traveled. This was what it probably came down to, his background and mine were too different, we'd never get over that, Jack being born and raised a Christian, his people Southerners, this making him a kind person at heart, while I was not. I was haute WASP, one of God's Frozen People, the kind of unfeeling person who ruins everything good she ever touches.

Home cooking in my family was simple, fresh vegetables and fruit, cracked crab from the Rainbow Pier. I missed my parents, my children, my own grandmothers, who'd gone to college. I missed the sunlight in California, its cool dry air.

Jack sat in a booth, me facing him. Limp, exhausted, I needed badly to at least put my head down on my folded arms but the surface of the Formica table had just been wiped, so I started pulling big bunches of paper napkins from the dispenser and lining them up along its edge.

What are you doing? Jack asked, as I lay my head down.

Resting.

You have to at least *try* to sit up, he said and now he was busy ordering me about in the stern no-nonsense baritone the kids and I call his Mr. Dickerson. Jack's Mr. Dickerson is the voice he uses in contract negotiations with assholes.

Can't, I said, reaching to pull out more napkins to make a better pillow. The awful microbial wetness was everywhere, reeking with that particularly sickening sweetish sour of an old bar towel.

Stop looking at me like that, I said, with my eyes closed. You should have come alone.

You need to eat something, he said.

No I don't, I said. Anyway, there's nothing to eat here except UFOs.

UFOs, Mr. Dickerson repeated, in the even voice that said no one was amused by anyone's self-invented three-letter acronym.

Unidentified Fried Objects, I said, eyes closed against the stinging glare, head cradled, speaking into the skin of my arm, face hurting, heart thudding, belly roiling from the existential pain of being dogless and my husband's hating me. As soon as you get home, I comforted myself, you can make yourself a nice cup of hot tea and take a sleeping pill.

We're out of milk, could you ask if they have those little plastic thingies of half-and-half? I said, my eyes still closed. Never mind, they use Coffee-Mate.

I was struggling to not let my bad feelings about the kennel woman prejudice me against all of Morgan County, West Virginia, being a place we'd all so deeply loved. You're not from here, I told myself, and small town people are clannish. Jack and I were what was wrong, he and I were from such a famous and important place, *California!* where they set TV shows about all its thin and expensive people, *California!* a place so *special* only an idiot would leave.

Californians were what was wrong with everything, people like us driving up here in our lawyer cars, bringing our upper-class dogs along, Californicating everything they touched. The PLU'd be eating in a place like this but not *sincerely.* We were tourists in our own lives just passing through, stopping here because we were momentarily charmed by all the quirky, down-home novelty.

I kept hearing what our friends back in town would be saying as word of what had happened to our dog went out: *Well, what can you expect from West Virginia?* No one except Jack and me would keep a place in a town like this, everyone we knew had houses in Vermont or The Vineyard or Aspen.

And I'd suddenly begun to actually *hate* the look of the off-brand ketchup squirters bought at the 99 Cent store down the road and the bottled-in-plastic Kraft ranch dressing sitting carelessly on each table. Now everything was bothering me, the grimy look of the too-long-ago painted walls, the obvious ill health of the customers, their bad teeth and obesity. This was conquered people, so defeated by their state's grinding poverty why not smoke and drink and eat nihilistically?

What are we doing here? I said to Jack.

Trying to get something to eat, he said studying the menu. I knew exactly what he was doing, trying to discover something that his food-snob bride might eat. The items on the menu had been typed, this sheet then sleeved in black-rimmed sticky plastic, exactly the touch sensation that gives us the word *tacky*.

No, I said, I mean us being here in the East? Why aren't we home with our own people, Jack? They at least halfway *get us* in Berkeley, I said, as it's there that we're known and needed and loved.

Jane, Jack said, *not now*. We're *torn down* from what we've been through and haven't eaten in a couple of days. You cannot reasonably discuss a topic such as this when you're half out of your mind with grief.

The prettier sister was now standing at our table bouncing her pencil on her pad while turned away, continuing her conversation with the fat man at the counter. She was, I knew, getting ready to tell us the specials, exactly the kind of information I was nowhere near well enough to hear.

The waitress glanced down and only then took a good look at us. Oh my god, what happened to you? she asked, staring from Jack to me and back again, eyes now wide and alarmed though the habit of her face still had her smiling.

You look *terrible!* she said, in her friendly, joking way. You look like your dog died.

Right there, I burst into tears, stood, rushed past the waitress, and ran out the door. I started home, truck lights on the highway picking me out then blurring by me. I pulled my tee shirt up to stuff its cloth in my mouth. The moon was coming up directly in front of me.

We don't belong here, I thought. It's the wrong town, in the wrong state, on the wrong side of the country.

The moon was rising. I could not stop sobbing. We aren't going to survive this, I said aloud, as I ran along the shoulder of the road, talking to the empty shape who'd fallen into heel and was now loping along beside me.

2

new world dog

The dog has no ambition, no self-interest, no desire
for vengeance, no fear other than that of displeasing.

GEORGES-LOUIS LECLERC,
COMTE DE BUFFON

bardo state

Of course you're messed up, Whistler was your baby. Someone said this to me in those first days after our dog died, but even as I was making noises of mild assent, I was also silently arguing, No, he was not. Whistler's being our dog meant both more and less than Jack's and my having a child together, in that the responsibility we'd taken on felt almost more grave than parenthood.

When you become a mother or a father, you expect that one day your son or daughter will stand eye-to-eye with you. In fact, achieving this equality is one of the main jobs of parenthood. But you get an animal with the compact that he'll be forever dependent on you, from this day forth, in sickness and in health.

The Universe had entrusted this dog to us and Whistler's dying in this completely avoidable way meant we'd fundamentally failed him. Dr. June Lawn, the local vet, told us bloat might be best described as what's called "gas" in humans, but in the anatomy of the dog it's often fatal. And in my flawed but all-encompassing wisdom, I had unerringly managed to pick the only kennel anywhere where they'd never heard of giving a dog in obvious gastric distress a dose of Maalox, which, as Dr. Lawn told us, *might* have given the kennel woman time to get our animal in for surgery, had the kennel woman been savvy enough to realize that that alone might save him.

But as much as I might sputter and deny it, this dog did come with all kinds of symbolic baggage. Jack and I had been together for years when we got Whistler, but it was only then that it felt like we were finally married. We are married! our having this dog said, we're married! And not to those we'd been married to before, or to other towns or domestic situations, but to one another and in this particular Here and Now.

And it is the dogwalking pace that really showed that place to me, that gave me the habitual chance to get to know its streets and roads and alleyways, its paths and trails. I'd only come to know my one or two intimate geographies by walking that land with him and I really *needed* to walk at Whistler's pace in order to witness the world as it really is.

Some people—to feel married—will buy a house or have a child as spiritual agent to offer tangible outward proof they're now committed to one another. Or they'll have the bans read, then stand in church in front of their community.

What Jack and I did was get an English springer spaniel.

And it was this dog who'd finally made us into the family we'd become: Whistler was unique, *sui generis*, displacing no other pet, bumping no kid from the birth order. He was, at base, just this really good dog, who had done nothing to deserve dying as he did, alone in a strange place, in terror, without comfort and in the most agonizing pain.

In those first few days without him, I'd lie upstairs in bed in West Virginia, immobilized, playing our dog's brief history out on the ceiling, how he'd begun life as the funniest, most playful, tumbling-over-and-around-things puppy, who liked to climb the mountain of his dad, then fall back into the pile of his littermates, who staggered here and there like a happy drunk, who then grew into a beautiful young dog, whose looks were actually elegant.

We were both in shock, we were not ourselves, I was benumbed by the loss of our dog, but believed I might shake apart in anger. I was furious with myself for not telling Jack how worried I'd been about boarding, for our not discussing it, for not even talking to one another about getting a housesitter, say. But mostly I was violently angry with the woman at the kennel.

I was also startled that my usual de-hexing rituals had not worked. These prayers, tiny actions, substitutions are the secret rites of the private ad hoc–ish religion in which my friend Alice Powers and I are the main communicants.

That Alice and I are both educated and sophisticated makes not one whit of difference in our practice. This religion of ours feels medieval, pagan, in that what it employs as sacred artifacts are the tackiest, kitschiest charms—lit candles, clanking necklaces, bracelets made of saints medals, thick stacks of plastic prayer cards— all that archaic-seeming stuff that's an outright embarrassment to those more thoughtfully entrenched in the august traditions in which Alice and I were raised. She is a churchgoing Roman Catholic, while I, after being delivered to my devoutly Episcopalian aunt, was required to attend catechism class and Girls' Friendly Society and a Eucharist service not only every Sunday but also on all holy days.

Only Alice and I understood how our secret little acts might work to keep our loved ones from harm and, at the very least, gave us something to do: attaching the St. Francis medals to our dogs' tags, then walking them over to the steps of National Cathedral to take part in the Blessing of the Animals.

So it's maybe only Alice who can truly understand how all this mind twisting and unraveling of a roped and spiraling spiritual puzzle *might* have worked magically and backward, even contrap-hobically, how my *not leaving* my dog at his frou-frou vets' might have even served to *actively* protect him. The original Wrong Dog Dream took place at Friendship, didn't it? which was no doubt a Sign or Portent?

And I'd at least *been trying* to act less hovering and protective, *trying* to take the sage advice offered by one or the other of our husbands when either Alice or I was acting too wrought-up over whatever was or wasn't going on with one of our animals or kids. Jane, Jack would say, you *do* understand that you cannot live and breathe for them, right? while Brian's most sound advice to Alice and me was this:

Ignore them.

⚅ ⚅ ⚅

How had all my scheming gone so disastrously wrong? I wondered, in that a nightmare like the Wrong Dog Dream almost always turns out *exactly* the way you want it to, with dreamer awakening to that flood of magical relief. The night dream of this worried variety is made to vex and opposite-away anxieties: You dream of the test you forgot to study for and this *always* means you're so well prepped you're going to go in there and kill it.

The terrifying dream is intended to work like this so you awaken to life as it really is: a constant miracle in which we're offered another chance to be with our loved ones.

But now that Jack and I saw what each of us had been privately worrying about had come exactly true, we were both sincerely spooked. Had the fact that we both had been doubling down on our worry somehow jinxed our dog by Double-X'ing the spot on the Treasure Map of Tragic Pet Loss?

I *knew* all this was crazy, knew it was insane to be so ruled by superstition, but since I'd already experienced an entire lifetime of terrible events that I carried like stones sewn into the hem of my dress—your father may well kill himself, your mother may well then go crazy—why shouldn't I go ahead and fall headfirst into cataclysmic sense of Front Page Headline tragedy?

It's how my mind works: My rational mind brings along its worry and goes and kneels in the same pew as prayer, doesn't everyone's? And I kneel and say I believe in one God, so forth, when I actually don't. What I believe is exactly what my dog believed, that—when it comes right down to it—none of us has much control over anything.

⚹ ⚹ ⚹

In the week that followed Whistler's dying, Jack and I were each so profoundly messed up that we simply couldn't talk or think straight, nor could we seem to stay out of bed. It was all we could do to brush our teeth. One or the other might take a shower, dress, try to accomplish some small thing. He stayed vertical long enough to unpack his bags from the trip. I unloaded half the dishwasher then quit when the work became too pointless.

We'd then each try to read our email, but the word was out and now came the stilted, awkward messages of dog-loss condolence, some of them from people we didn't know very well, those who hadn't known Whistler. The awkwardness of the notes bothered me; they were well-meaning, I knew, but almost every word they used was deeply and profoundly *wrong.*

We'd talk on the phone to our kids, to Keltie and Heather and John in Jack's office, to Trish, and we'd make our voices sound strong and even booming to impress them all with how well we were doing. Yes, we said, we were taking a little time but we were better day by day.

We were better day by day, we said, when the truth was we weren't better at all. We were not better, we knew, and when the phone rang it was a chore to go answer it, though answer it we had to or they'd worry about us. Talking on the phone was its own grim chore, so we took turns.

We were not getting better, as being better meant we'd be moving forward into another country, the land of the Future, but this was where our dog Whistler could not follow, so neither Jack nor I was willing to yet go.

We'd awaken each day vowing that this would be the day when we'd begin to make a little headway, but by midafternoon, the misery and exhaustion would come to find one of us who, newly overwhelmed, would go stand by the other, leaning against a bookcase to say, Want to come to bed and hold me? and—since feeling needed was better than feeling blank and worthless and furious—the other would simply arise and go.

We lay in bed, we held each other, we sobbed, we rested on our backs. We replayed the whole of Whistler's life with us, saying, Remember how he always . . . ? all the while staring at the ceiling, and as we did one or the other would begin to silently cry, tears welling up, seeping out, spilling from our eyes, sliding down the sides of our faces, wetting our ears, our necks and hair, the pillowcases.

We weren't indulging our grief, nor were we wallowing: We were simply helpless to do otherwise. We now were growing ashamed of how terrible we kept on feeling, now we'd started hiding how difficult all this had become, our grief now threatening to turn darker, as it went underground, turning into something older, angrier and more secretive.

❅   ❅   ❅

Jack's unspoken fear of leaving Whistler was the reason he always stumped to take him with us when we flew home to California. At fifty pounds, our dog was too large for an under-the-seat carrier, but because he was a calm and serene traveler who liked riding in cars, we were comfortable shipping him in his crate in the baggage compartment.

Then the airlines changed their rules. This happened the year after that most dog-awesome of Augusts, when we had Whistler with us first at Squaw where Jack and I both taught at the writers' conference, then in the foothills of the Sierra, then went to stay with our friends Gary Snyder and Carole Koda on San Juan Ridge. It was there at Squaw we first saw our dog's ability to leap through the tall grasses of the gold-green bunchgrass meadow, his bounding so high you could see exactly how the springer got his name.

But one of the airlines had carelessly lost some animals who'd been left too long in their crates on the tarmac at some hub, either in the bitter cold at O'Hare or in the blistering heat of Dallas-Fort Worth, and the unfortunate deaths of those four dogs got such wide press, becoming national headline news, which so devastated every traveling pet owner in the United States, that the rules were changed overnight. After that, during the winter and summer months, any time of extreme temperatures, the airlines would only accept those animals who could travel with you in the cabin.

Our tandem and oddly entwined anxiety was such that we'd automatially perk up and listen to every tragic dog story, to any anecdote of risk: dog loss, dog death, dog injury or infirmity, every dog-related close call. Our friends shared these stories with us, we told them in return, all of us struggling with the thought that—even as our children were growing into independence and self-sufficiency—that loving our dogs as mindlessly as we did had placed us back there in what felt like those newborn days of extreme emotional vulnerability where an entire household is ruled by the needs of its most helpless member.

And now that Whistler had actually died—though we each were still struggling with our need to accept this—Jack and I each felt spooked and doomed and shattered, as if loving our dog, then losing him in exactly the manner each of us had separately imagined, had somehow subtracted from our lives every particle of luck we'd ever managed to accrue.

We felt more than haunted, felt—in fact—trapped by cruel Fate, as if all this had been foretold. Our loss was not only predicted by the Wrong Dog Dream, it was probably even preordained. The dream said this one true thing: Some day you will have your dog no more.

Our dogs, unlike our children and grandchildren, are not likely to outlive us—how could Jack and I have been so dim as to not remember this? Nothing, no loss he'd ever endured, not his divorce from Vic nor the death of his parents, had marked Jack as had his watching his dog Rags getting hit by a car, in that it took him decades to get over it. Why had we done this to ourselves? when it was so obvious that neither of us was psychologically equipped to deal with the loss of our dog?

And now each was struggling to make our own personal kind of sense of this tragic accident's senselessness. I examined our differences from the people we now lived among. Like so many West Virginians, the kennel woman was shrewd instead of smart, only canny enough to half understand us, putting our differences down to our book learning and picking up on my intellectual condescension. She understood that I could easily use a thousand words in explaining her, no doubt got that I could so easily diagnose the socioeconomic causes of so much of what was going wrong with her crappy life and all that now rippled out from that. West Virginians were once a self-sufficient people, who—because of coal mining—felt almost entirely dispossessed by the outside commercial interests who were ruining the state's natural beauty even as they siphoned off its staggering mineral riches.

But if I'd misjudged her, so too had she fundamentally misjudged me, and it seemed true enough to say she and I did not inhabit the same moral universe. I was now blaming all of Appalachia for the loss of Whistler, blaming its deep-seated culture of insularity and suspicion of outsiders that helped create this hopelessly embittered person. She blamed us. She blamed us for our Otherness. This is why she felt justified in feeling no contrition.

I was thinking caste, class, power, proximity to power, while Jack, according to his lifelong practice of Buddhist teaching and instruction, was becoming ever more high-minded and forgiving, which was often just so monumentally irritating! When he offered the opinion that I shouldn't call her anymore, I nodded to agree but my nodding only meant I'd now call her when he wasn't there to witness it.

As I sat propped against pillows with my laptop on the bed upstairs, Jack sent me an email from his computer downstairs, quoting Judith Butler:

> We are simply undone by one another, and if we're not, we're missing something. If this seems so clearly the case with grief, it is only because it was already the case with desire. *One does not always stay intact.*

Italics mine, Jack had added.

Truly, I thought, we were undone by our losing our dog. We were simply no longer ourselves, no longer whole, the world had tilted and our place—at least here in Morgan County—no longer felt secure.

If we'd loved it here, I thought, this was because we didn't know the first thing about these people, having been insulated from having to deal with them by our living on a farm run by Tom and Katherine and Moochie, three good, sweet, smart, kind people who happened to like us. Everyone else was like the kennel woman, I guessed, purposefully ignorant and hating Jack and me for the books we read and wrote, published and collected, books that stood in accusation of them, in that these books told of the Outside World.

I was now dry-eyed. I now stared soberly at the ceiling, trying to read the past in the back-up mirror: Hazel's birthday is March 21st, the first day of spring. Why hadn't we at least phoned the airline to ask if Whistler could fly with us? And what was the matter with me that I'd been unwilling to take the ninety minutes it required to drive our dog back to the city so he could be at Friendship, which was an animal hospital! where, if he'd gotten bloat, they might have operated immediately and saved his life?

And why was I sitting out in the country by myself working on yet another of my projects? In it I was again rehashing the events of my childhood, which my older brother was now revisionistically characterizing as not all that bad, really, saying, Well, they were at least amusing, and let's face facts here: No one molested us. No one beat us with a wooden spoon.

Why was I still fixed on my sodden personal history instead of putting the past behind me and going out to live an actual life?

                                                    ℵ ℵ ℵ

Eva was still at college a ten hours' drive away but kept calling to say she was coming down if we didn't begin to sound like we were feeling way, way better. Had we actually gotten it together to shop for groceries?

I just couldn't help the way I sounded. The moment I was on the phone with Eva, I'd just really need to launch into my sociological views of how the deformed soul of the kennel woman came to be that way, going on about how the poverty of the mind and body and spirit will in fact defeat you.

Then I'd go on some more about how the Fundamentalist Christian Right is, in fact, our enemy, how it's become a movement in which embittered racism self-justifies, how they are waging a cultural war on anyone brown or black or tan and how so much of their hatefulness is directed at us, as women.

Okay, Mom, my daughter said. Could you put Jack on?

Well, it honestly is all interconnected, honey, I said as I wandered about looking for Jack. I found him outside, refilling his birdfeeders, handed him my cell phone, and went back in. I knew the two of them would now discuss me. Eva was probably right then saying, Notice how my mom doesn't really talk on the phone but just goes off on these rants?

I could hear her worrying aloud over her mom's being so fringy and out there she couldn't even react normally even when our dog died, in that her mom would always feel the need to say all these weird and abstract things that had nothing to do with dogs? Ever notice, my daughter would ask, how much my mother talks?

By Saturday midmorning Eva's more reasonable parent was recovered enough to walk to the Sheetz to buy the *New York Times* and a sandwich and I was sitting upright in bed, laptop in hand, committing private electronic acts while appearing to be working. What I was doing was secretly trolling through the mug shots of every dog in every shelter within a five-state radius.

This behavior—like any electronic addiction—felt pushed and driven. It felt twisted and solipsistic, like I was looking at porn. I was feeling as flat as Muffin, so numb and depressed it was only in looking at the images on the dog adoption sites that I could feel a short little zinging blast of interest. My interest, however, would last only the tiniest piece of a second, no longer than it took for me to click from image to image.

If you'd asked what I was doing, I'd have said: None of your business, or more precisely, Won't you please go away and leave me to my robotic misery? I would never have admitted aloud what I was really doing: looking for my dog Whistler.

Which did not make sense, as I understood. I understood this even as I went on clicking through the faces of random dogs, thinking, not you, not you, not you. I didn't know what I was looking for, only that I'd know it when I came to it.

Humane societies and shelters in poor Appalachian states, however, just don't happen to have an overabundance of show-quality purebred AKC-registered English springer spaniels that have been given up for adoption. And I wasn't a good person, evidently, since I didn't want one of the truly miscreant-looking English springer spaniels you came to on springer rescue sites, dogs who were obviously the same breed as Whistler except they looked deformed.

I wasn't a good person and my heart had hardened against what now felt like Dogs, Plural, in that I felt nothing, no twinge at all as I looked at face after face, all the while going not you, not you, not you.

I went on blazing through the online dog snapshots the whole while Jack was out, staying away from the springer rescue sites, because the dogs there would sometimes be almost-Whistler looking, Whistler-ish enough to bring on that old Wrong Dog sensation, which was completely disquieting. I kept waiting to be hit by the feeling that a dog possessed enough of my own real dog to be some kind of help to us.

This dog-shaped emptiness of Jack's and mine had become a palpable lack, a dark cold absence-of-presence that followed us everywhere. It lay down on the rug next to Jack's desk or would curl heavily into place at the foot of our bed.

I knew Whistler was gone, yet could still feel his proximity to me, I felt him there, as if I might catch a glimpse of him if only I turned my head fast enough.

I'd felt this same sense of physical presence after my mother died the year Noah was three. She was under hospice care and died in my house in a back bedroom. The sense that my mother's spirit remained hovering right there where she left our physical world was comforting, I'd feel it most strongly in that little room where she'd breathed her last breath. I liked to sew in the rocking chair I'd moved in there while she was dying, rocking while sewing binding on a baby blanket. I was using a silk thread so glossy and smooth it offered no resistence as I pulled it through the fabric, making small careful hypnotic *X*s, knowing that by the time I'd finished the blanket my mother's earthly spirit would have moved a little ways away, to stand at the little distance where it now continues to reside, ready to be summoned in time of need.

That strong feeling, the very physical sense of my mother's spiritual presence, lasted several days, then gradually faded. In this it resembled that period of time so honored by Christian liturgy, those hours from Friday through Sunday of Holy Week, between Christ's death and His Resurrection.

In Buddhism this same transition is called the Bardo State, that patch of timely existence linking a being on two sides of the invisible seam marking the boundary between a soul's two expressions, the life it's just left and its next incarnation.

It was my friend Brenda Hillman, the poet, who explained the Bardo State to me. She once wrote a poem called "Cleave and Cleave" that's been important to me over the years, a poem about how these two words mirror one another, yet whose meanings are direct opposites, the word *cleave* to mean to bind lastingly together even as the word *cleave* also means to violently separate.

Both love and grief simply sunder us, cleave us from ourselves, break us to pieces, atomizing us as individuals so we can be remade. I could simply *not* not do what I was doing, was simply too destroyed and didn't have enough personhood to resist the sight of these dogs who might give me back to myself.

My behavior now reminded me of the Bardo State I entered in falling in love with Jack, that transition, in which I was no longer autonomous. Jack and I—each encumbered by our own separate and oh-so-complicated lives—fell dramatically in love over the course of one long weekend in New York, where we'd each found out the other was also visiting: serendipity, the happy accident, and it did seem like something The Fates had arranged.

Given this one out-of-town opportunity, we behaved in that end-of-the-world-ish way, this to say wrecklessly. All this felt cataclysmic, like we were participating in the deluge that came to erase our previous selves. We'd been falling in love gradually as we'd worked together on the book I'd written and he had published, but now that book was out in the world and we no longer had the work-related excuse to keep seeing one another, as we both so clearly wanted to do. Discovering the other was going to be in New York, we'd made a plan to have breakfast at his hotel, then to go together to a museum, which is the kind of date Jack will always make with friends and authors and colleagues. While in the cab up Sixth Avenue on our way to the Met, he reached over and took my hand and I essentially never went back to my own hotel.

Those actions—his taking my hand, his then leaning over to kiss me—completely altered the course of not only our two lives but all of those with whom either of us was intimately connected. Jack and I took all this seriously, as he and I are both serious people in no way talented at infidelity. His first gift to me was an ivory Knot of Entanglement, the Buddhist symbol acknowledging all the myriad ways we participate in life and are only alive as part of our boundless and interconnected circles of mutual dependencies. Attached to it by satin ribbon was a house key.

He and I are serious people and because others were involved, it occurred to us to think seriously of what we were doing. We imagined alternatives to the course we appeared to be choosing: We might acknowledge that these things happen, then do the more adult and less disruptive thing, that is, fly home to Berkeley vowing never to see one another again. We might have done so had we not fallen in love.

In a state of joy I'll feel strong and certain, as if my personhood has quietly coalesced into its most solidly three-dimensional aspect. In joy, I'm sorry for nothing that's ever happened, as even the tragedy of losing my parents gave me the story I need to tell, which turned out to be a larger story than the one about the three sad orphans.

What Jack and I felt was much more dire than joy, as that word imparts the sense of peace and balance—we felt blown down, falling crazily in love, each undone by passionate feeling, all of this heady and exciting, not to be missed, yet shot through with existential danger and risk.

I was so terrified at what we were about to embark on I'd have rather been a dog. I was about to lose my house, my home, almost all my friends, my social standing. I'd be talked about, like I'd been orphaned all over again.

Dogs don't fall in love, nor does their love wax and wane. Instead they love as we all might hope to: consistently, day in, day out, week after week, loving steadily year after year, dogs being naturally so much better at the practice of joy than you and I can ever hope to be.

§ § §

Saturday, early afternoon. Hearing my husband on the stairs I quickly click away from the site where I've been staring at the hypothetical dogs. I'm guessing he's coming upstairs to tell me I must eat lunch.

Look what I found, holding a sheet of paper out to me.

I drag my eyes from the ghost dogs to glance at what Jack's holding out to me: a soggy sheet of heavily inked typing paper printed with the still-wet image of a smiling black puppy. Tongue lolling, starburst of white on his chest, this pup standing tall on long straight hind legs, peering out over the top of a yellow plastic laundry basket.

This is a dog that looks so little like an English springer spaniel that it might be a different species.

What is it? I ask.

What they have so much of around here, Jack says. Greyhound, obviously, a little border collie. Maybe a touch of Lab?

The puppy looks ungainly, head narrow enough to call arrow-shaped, thin face dominated by a nose so long it appears ridiculous. And those negligible little greyhound earflaps?

Looks intelligent, doesn't he? Jack says.

You think? I say.

Do you like him? Jack says.

Do you?

Fourteen weeks, Jack goes on. Last of a litter of four born in the shelter, his mom dropped off pregnant there—someone's just adopted her so now he's there all alone. And get this, he's only a few miles away, down past the turnoff on 522 at the Morgan County Humane Society.

I'm now staring openly at Jack. Let me get this straight, I say, you are seriously considering our going out to adopt this dog?

He's only a few minutes away, Jack says. How would it hurt to drop in to have a casual little visit with him?

Jack, I say, we're not well enough to drop in for a casual visit with some puppy in some shelter. Our dog died less than a week ago, we're still traumatized! Our judgement is impaired, this is exactly why they tell you No Major Changes.

My kids' father is a psychoanalyst. No Major Changes is what he's always said, No Major Changes being what all Helping Professionals will tell you in almost any interesting situation.

But now Jack's face is settling, jaw tightening imperceptibly as it does whenever he feels challenged. Jack's tired of being told what to do by The Experts. He has just dug in.

I think we should look at him, Jack says.

All right, I say, but if we go meet this dog, you do realize we'll be bringing him home with us?

It's a beautiful spring day, Jack says, wildflowers out, great day for a hike in the state park at Cacapon. There's no harm in dropping in at the shelter along the way.

All right, I say, but I need to wash my face.

He really is handsome, isn't he? Jack says, showing me the page again.

I'd more call it cute, I tell him, to not say what I'm really thinking, which is: Well, no, not really. He's actually ill-proportioned, he looks awkward, in that his legs are too long and spindly, also his eyes don't seem to match.

But I say none of this. I say none of it because Jack has already fallen in love with this dog and cannot see the first thing about what he objectively looks like.

I need to do something about my hair, I say. And I guess I could shower . . . ?

Of course, he says, and while you're doing that, I'll go fill out the online application. They suggest your doing it online in case several parties are interested in the same dog and—

Several parties? I say, unable to keep the skepticism from my tone.

—so our application will appear at the front of the electronic queue. What are you laughing at?

I'm just thinking we might require some new word to explain this new dog of ours, that he's the runt, the leftover. Which makes him, what? The Worst in Show?

I don't know what you're talking about, Jack says. This is objectively one good-looking dog.

Sure he is, I say. You do realize the kids will be making some massive deal of our getting a dog like this, it's demonstrating for all time how messed up we are. We're so messed up, in fact, that we'll go fill the round hole of our gaping need with any square peg.

So, Jack says.

Which makes us as desperate as that old friend of your dad's stopping at the Safeway on his way home from his mom's funeral and meeting the woman standing behind him in the checkout whom he married two weeks later.

They'll get over it, Jack says.

returning the gaze

As I was frantically scrolling through online dog sites upstairs, looking for that one face that seemed to be looking back at me, Jack was downstairs—as I was now finding out—trying to literally replace our dog, which hadn't actually occurred to me. He'd been looking up springer breeders online, searching for the pup whose DNA might be a close match to Whistler's, then emailing them to ask about upcoming litters.

He'd contacted our same breeder out in PG County, finding that Whistler's sire had died, while they still had the mom. She'd had a litter of six pups earlier that month, sadly all now spoken for.

Jack told me he'd started dog shopping for himself and for me, of course, but largely because of Alice Vetter. Alice was our landlady at our new place in town and had designed our garden apartment in her house on Embassy Row to be rented exclusively to people who owned dogs.

Such a nice place, Jack smiled as we went to the car, and we don't want the Vetters to throw us out.

It was becoming obvious to each of us that we really were on our way to go get this odd-looking, long-legged, and maybe wall-eyed puppy, that we were not only doing this sight unseen, but that there was probably no force on earth that could stop us.

The world that day had dawned cold, dark, unstable, another morning awash with all my age-old terrors—what Jack and I were maybe doing was simply seeing what we could accomplish in trying to turn the dreary ship of life around.

My father was a tall, elegant, soft-hearted man who could not bear the sight of his children with their feelings hurt and so would take us directly to the pound at the slightest provocation, a new puppy or kitten being his answer to any kind of childhood hurt or disappointment.

When my mom was in the hospital having me, our dad began to fret about my older brother feeling left out. Hank, whose birthday is eight days after mine, was turning three, so our father took him to the Berkeley pound, and they came home with a new black puppy.

Our maternal grandmother, up from Glendale to help out, took one look at them as they walked in the front door and said: John, you will either be taking that dog back where you found him or you'll be driving me to the train.

I don't know if our grandmother left in a huff or not. I do know we kept that dog, as this was the black Lab we had at Boulder Creek. Doc so loved our mom that he'd jungle-crawl along the top of the couch, then dive down in order to get between her and the child trying to sit next to her.

❧ ❧ ❧

You can tell so much about a culture by the way it treats its weakest members. So too you can judge the heart of a people by the care with which it treats its animals.

If you want to know about Morgan County, you go to its Humane Society, that modest, no-frills, but beautifully run facility lying a couple of miles east of town. We'd first heard about the shelter from

Paul, the fourteen-year-old son of Tom and Katherine Truitt. Paul volunteered there after school, accumulating the hours he needed for his Bar Mitzvah.

Driving to the shelter we passed the house of the woman with the kennel, where a clutch of teenaged boys sat idly on the porch, smoking and looking very bored and a little mean.

Raising that lot in this town would be a thankless task, Jack said.

And she's alone, I said. Without backup and lacking time and energy to work a boy.

In saying *work a boy* I was quoting our friend Wendell Berry, who says a teenaged boy is that creature who requires not only hard physical labor but someone to work alongside him while he's doing it, to demonstrate to that boy that you do not actually die of it. It is only hard physical labor performed hour after hour—exactly the kind of work you're not certain you will survive—that syphons off the energy that can turn so easily destructive.

It's often only by tiring him completely out, Wendell says, that you can keep a boy from getting in trouble.

Going to have to give up on all that, Jack said, smiling at me sideways. We need to put this behind us.

I know, I said. I do know, Jack, I repeated, and if I had holy water I'd sprinkle it in their direction. If I had holy water and believed in that kind of . . . ? In deference to Jack's sensibilities I don't say *shit*.

But I was also offering silent benediction, thinking, Bless them and keep them, O Lord, all the days of their lives and untie the bonds of my fury at her so I can forgive her for it's only in forgiveness that I can let those people go . . .

I had to give up being mad because I'm a person so poorly equipped at being angry that it makes me almost physically ill. I am no better at being angry, really, than I am at drinking alcohol, to which I am probably allergic, as each makes me feel just as wildly insane.

Over the final years of my marriage to my kids' dad, wine-fueled anger was our cocktail of choice. A mutual anger such as ours— explosive, smoldering, inexhaustable, compounding—tends to become its own closed system, feeding off itself as it self-perpetuates. At the end it was only when he and I were really angry that we felt completely alive.

We were angry at one another for not turning out to be the other's salvation, also mad at ourselves for being duped into indulging in such a crazy expectation. But we were each furiously disappointed, as well, at the way the larger world seemed to treat us with bland indifference. Where, we each privately thought, is all that recognition that's probably due me? where is my fame? where are my riches? where's the proof I seem to need of my importance?

So my falling in love with this man, a Buddhist who's so little moved by such outward signs and superficial concerns, has been such a huge relief. Jack is repressed in no way but is by nature so slow to anger it's been to me like a balm in Gilead.

℘   ℘   ℘

A quarter to two on a Saturday afternoon and now Jack and I are each quietly panicking that we won't get to the shelter ahead of the huge crowd already probably amassing, all clamoring to adopt the only puppy in any shelter anywhere around.

We see him as soon as we turn in and pull up to park, there through the open fencing, several pens back. He's standing on his long hind legs against the chicken wire of his enclosure, taller, larger, older than the one in the photograph but—even at twenty yards— the same pup without question.

We're in such a rush to stop the car, set the brake, click off seat-belts, open doors, get out, ready to dash into the office ahead of the rest that, at first, we don't really notice that the parking lot's empty aside from us.

Hey! we call out as we go in, We're here! We emailed you? We're the ones who applied for the black puppy online?

Oh, why, sure, one of the women says. The two women who work there are both big, older, kindly, also each keenly sympathetic as our poor sad story of dog woe comes spilling out, how we've now been dogless for almost a week, how we're barely holding on, not coping, really not being able to stand it, how we need a dog to walk in order to get out of bed, how we have this irrepressible need to adopt this dog, who was born in this shelter, and whose mother has been adopted and he's alone, as well, and so obviously *in need of us too!*

Noble looking, isn't he? Jack says as we walk with the two women out toward the enclosure, and now my husband's voice sounds buoyed up again by happiness, also confident and awed by his return to his usual state of good fortune.

Doesn't he look like exactly what you'd draw if you were trying to draw a picture of a dog? Jack asks.

Trying to draw a dog? I think, *and being only marginally successful?*

And while the other dogs in the shelter are making an enormous racket, all barking their heads off, our puppy is watching us with an expression that's both calm and expectant, like he's been there all this time patiently waiting, never doubting that we would come.

⚮ ⚮ ⚮

Recent research into dog cognition merely proves scientifically what we already intuitively know: It's the dog's ability to hold our gaze that formed that early bond in the most ancient world in which the ancient peoples first brought dogs home as co-equals to live with them.

An animal's gaze, when directed at our faces, allows us to feel he can be trusted, as we believe we can know what this animal is feeling by watching him. We seem to read one another in this way, to hold one another in intimate, cross-species regard.

"Their gaze implies a state of mind [and] attention," writes Alexandra Horowitz, in her recent groundbreaking book *Inside of a Dog: What Dogs See, Smell and Know.* "Look a dog in the eyes," she goes on, "and you get the definite feeling that he is looking back . . . The dog is both paying attention to you, and, very possibly, paying attention to your attention." (p. 139)

Dogs, in some profound way, seem not only to look at us, but also to actually see us, so we may feel they know something about us that we have ourselves forgotten. This, I think, is what that is: Our dogs recognize you and me as fellow animals. What kind of animal are we? We are *their* animals, of course.

The animal in the wild—be it wolf or cougar—is incurious about us in this way, having no real wish to understand who or what we are and so will look away. They look away because gaze among predators reads as a challenge to this animal's dominance. If we stare at an animal in the wild and he stares back, he may well read this look as a threat to his dominion over what he feels is his rightful territory. He feels that way because it is.

And it's right there in that flux on the border of the wild that the rules grow vague and it's here the situation can become dangerously unstable. We don't look at a wild animal because we don't want to be known by him, rather, we want to be as rock or tree to them and not seem like either predator or prey. We do not own the wild and cannot win there except, perhaps, by destroying it.

We do not own the wild, yet we still do understand animal rules instinctively, remembering from those ancient days when we, as human beings, still wordlessly inhabited that wilder place and were more closely tuned in to our animal natures. This is how we know intuitively, without being tutored, to drop our eyes to avoid staring at the dog who might be vicious. All this happens in our bodies, long before we sort it out as rational exercise.

The wolf or cougar is the true cousin of our own dog or cat. Since no species barrier divides them, they can and will freely mate and bare fertile offspring, so perhaps one of the primary differences between an animal at home and the one in the wild is our ability to trust our pets. This trust begins in our ability to hold one another in neutral and intimate gaze in which neither is dominant nor subservient.

And we do seem to need the reassurance our pets offer us, needing this because our animals speak to us in that most ancient and wordless vocabulary of scent, sound, nuance, gesture, that's closer to music or dance than it is to language. We know one another by an almost wordless telepathy that offers us a bridge back to our more true selves, when we still confidently belonged to that older, better nation where we all began.

℘ ℘ ℘

This new dog of ours was not only long-legged, he was long of body, also big chested, and all this was typical of what is known as the West Virginia porch hound. This is not an actual breed.

We named him Thiebaud as we were telling the women at the shelter, adding, We always name our dogs after great American painters, saying this as if there had, by now, been scores of them.

After T. Bone Burnett? one woman asked. He's a painter too?

After Wayne Thiebaud, we said, the California painter of seascapes, townscapes, all those gorgeous desserts?

They nod agreeably, either recognizing the name or not, hard to tell, as West Virginians are often shrewd, knowledgeable, if disinclined to tell you so, particularly if they're feeling your worldly condescension. And what is famous to you in your own little part of the cosmos may be completely mystifying to folks just one county over.

We're telling them about Whistler, as they both nod for us and the other collects the $45 adoption fee and arranges a date for us to take him to be neutered. They've already decided they're waiving the forty-eight-hour waiting period so we can take our dog home!

The forty-eight-hour waiting period, as they explained, was designed to ward off exactly the kind of blind impulsivity Jack and I were both exhibiting, but since we're both there and seemingly in this thing together . . . ?

We now had Thiebaud, he was ours, this long-legged, colt-like puppy who trotted out to the car with us, got into the passenger side of the front with me willingly enough, but then revolted. He pulled up short as soon as Jack started the engine, affronted by the sound and by the new and sudden motion. It was like he'd never ridden in a car before, which—to think of it—he maybe hadn't.

What the . . . ? our dog seemed to say. He was standing rigidly, back feet in my lap, tail in my face, front paws on the dash, haunches pressed back and hard up against my chest, nose so far forward it seemed to nearly touch the windshield.

You saved our lives, I told the two women, talking out the rolled-down window, past dog rump, through dog fur and dog tail. Really, I said. We might not have even survived.

That's one lucky dog, one of the women said.

He'd been kenneled too long, the other added. They get a little iffy when they grow up without being in someone's home.

Thank you so much, I said. We don't just don't have words to thank you.

Why, sure. Our pleasure, they said to us, waving. So long, Tee Bone, they called as we drove away, waving and waving: Bye bye! Tee Bone, they called out, have a happy life!

৪

home again

৪

When Odysseus returns to Ithaca after his long and terrible journey, he first appears as a beggar, so bedraggled his own servants don't know him. Even his wife, Penelope, finds him so altered by time and hardship that she can't trust him to be the man he claims and so devises riddles to test him. It's only his dog Argus who offers him acceptance, and, in lowering his ears and wagging his tail in recognition, demonstrates to Odysseus that he's finally made it home.

And in what is one of the stoical Odysseus's very few displays of emotion, he cries as he and Argus each see the other in that deep way. Odysseus weeps not only for all the years he's been away but for missing the young dog who grew old as he patiently awaited his master's return, it being Argus alone who never faltered in his belief this would happen.

People change, as Homer tells us, writing nearly fifteen hundred years ago. People change while a dog's love is immutable, as constant and luminous as the Dog Star, brightest in the sky. People change as our dogs do not, so we depend on our animals to reassure us that we are the people we once were. It's as if our animals lock onto our better selves and so forever bring that out in us, trusting us to be what we originally were before life did what it will do to each of us.

And it does sometimes feel like it's this relationship that's key, the only one that's simple. It is only in our animals' affection that you and I too remain constant and forever impervious to Time.

⚜ ⚜ ⚜

Tee was already three and a half months old when we got him, more than half grown, taller than Whistler and nearly as heavy. Because his mother was dumped at the pound, he'd never lived inside anybody's house and so had lost out on that stability offered by early human contact. This dog needed the loving, orderly home life Jack and I were now promising to provide him.

Tee was entirely confident out-of-doors but either inside our car or a building he'd become instantly confused by the confines of an interior space, as if the man-made world was inherently strange to him.

Our dog spent the next two days in the construction of the map of our place in West Virginia. This process is described by the animal scientist John Bradshaw in his recent *Dog Sense: How the New Science of Dog Behavior Can Make You a Better Friend to Your Pet* (p. 239–240), who tells how a dog employs sight, sound, smell, and his acute auxiliary sense of olfactory "taste" to do this mapping, committing each new landscape to multilayered, multisensory, contextual memory, into which Time is compounded and layered.

It may have been that Tee was searching the corners looking for Eva's cat, Phoebe, who—as ever—was in hiding. There suddenly appeared Jack's evident message to Thiebaud: affixed by magnet to the fridge right at our new dog's eye-height was a postcard reading, CATS ARE NOT IMPORTANT.

⚜ ⚜ ⚜

If grief stops the clocks, turns Time into that thick substance it feels nearly impossible to trudge through, joyousness has the opposite effect. Tee's first job in our household was to enact his own boundless sense of JOY, to get the moments of our day to tick forward once again.

We really needed him in this regard. As we'd explained to the women at the shelter, we were depending on him to keep us up and out of bed, to free us from the prison that gloomy room had become. He was there to remind us how much work a rambunctious puppy is. We had no choice but to do this work. If we weren't up for what it took to care for this dog, we'd have to take him back.

The Greeks named Necessity the mother of all Three Fates. This new dog of ours—acquired out of plain, grim need—seemed to bring us the message of how it's Necessity that will swing open the hinge that shows us the present moment might be built on the Past, but also predicates the Future.

Our lives without Thiebaud become almost instantly unthinkable, which did not mean we were missing Whistler less, only that we were now mourning him in a more healthy, active way, missing him in every step we took as we walked those same trails with this new dog, who most likely—because of his astonishing time-layered senses—could still faintly track him.

The Three Fates, named also the Daughters of Necessity, had seemingly arranged to give us the dog who was Whistler's opposite: Tee was humorous, stable, not one whit jealous of his place in the New World he was asked to join, easily confident he'd find his rightful slot in the hierarchy.

Affectionate, overtly sociable, he seemed on a mission to win all people over to him, sure he could accomplish this if he just patiently took them one by one. He was like a Bill Clinton–type politician, not to be satisfied until everyone had fallen hard for him. Whistler's sense of self-pride? That measured cool aloofness? Not Thiebaud, being dignified simply never having occurred to him.

For a long-kenneled animal, Thiebaud had miraculously become this sensible, intelligent, exceedingly trusting and friendly dog. Like any foundling, he excelled at self-suffiency, suffering not at all when left alone. Of course I identified with him: All orphans are like this, we take no one's affection for granted, we never assume anyone will like us, but once we're convinced we can trust you, we'll fall even ridiculously in love with you. We do it because we're so relieved and grateful.

But it was Jack our dog latched on to as his first ardent attachment, which made sense since each has the same talent for happiness. Happiness is probably like any other gift—dancing, say, or being musically inclined? and coming easily only to some. Then there are the others—and I am one, my dog Whistler was another—who will simply have to work at it.

Thiebaud was interested in everything Jack did as long as they could be together: sitting quietly outside watching as Jack looked after his fruit trees or restocked his birdfeeders. Then, inside—after running a few frenetic interior exploratory laps around the big room he seemed to take as a dogtrack—Tee lay with Jack on the couch, his small ears flicking back and forth, seeming to really listen to the Metropolitan Opera being broadcast on West Virginia Public Radio every Saturday afternoon.

Tee had what Dog Maida would describe as the characteristically beta personality, but Jack—who discounts our current requirement that we dismissively label and judge—called it his dog's good Southern manners.

Thiebaud was both patient and deferential, sitting by his full bowl watching until both Jack and I were seated at the dinner table. It was because of our dog that Jack and I began our now long-standing practice of reading a different grace from a little book we have of ecumenical blessings, this so Tee—in hearing the somewhat singsong cadences of prayer always ending in the word *Amen*—would get the signal that he too was now invited to eat.

Thiebaud had simply demanded that we come to life, saying you need to grab a leash, need to step outside into Jack's fragrant little orchard where the pear and cherry and apple were now budding, need to notice how the the hillside beyond the shed has gone crazy with wildflowers: bluebell, cowslip, adder's-tongue, trout lily.

Over the short time we'd been away in California, spring had riotously arrived, making our little patch of Morgan County into a whole new and beautiful world.

Look at this! our new dog seemed to say: How amazing to be alive!

⅋ ⅋ ⅋

There are two kinds of West Virginia jokes, the derogatory ones told from outside the clan—these will be the ones by the city sophisticates, those folks who bolster their own shaky sense of who they are by heaping contempt on the rural poor. The punchline will reference incest or maybe *The Dairy Queen*.

But for the outsider joke, there is often the insider corollary, whereby the members of this vilified group—knowing exactly what the world thinks of them—all pull together and here you'll feel toolmarks of an agrarian people engaged in a traditional way of life that has changed little over centuries and is proud of its self-reliance: How can you tell you're a *real* West Virginian? You got jumper cables in your truck but it's your old lady who can *really* handle them.

The West Virginia porch hound is one of the insider jokes: Not exactly AKC, as the saying goes, more whatcha get when you cross whatever wanders up on the porch with whatcha already got.

And this is the history of Thiebaud's not-really-a-breed: In a rural place—with great distances between houses—dogs are kept outside, they hang out on the porch, their barking being the first signal someone's driving up your lane, which is why a barking dog is known as a country doorbell.

In Morgan County the ordinary mongrel mix often shows the

long legs and small ears of the greyhound and it was this preponderance of greyhound that so easily showed in Thiebaud.

He had those long, well-muscled if almost spindling looking legs, arrow-shaped head that looks aerodynamically designed, tiny flicking ears that seemed—in contrast to the extravagance of Whistler's—like Post-its stuck on as afterthought. But unlike the real greyhound, whose fur is so short it looks sprayed on, Tee had a real coat of two-inch fur that bunched at his shoulders, an inheritance from the border collie the shelter woman told us was so obvious in his mom's makeup.

There's all this greyhound in the crossbreeds of the Eastern Panhandle because there's a racetrack at Charles Town, twenty miles from Berkeley Springs. Racing dogs are famously exploited, treated almost as poorly as those bred for fighting, except dog racing is legal. These dogs are raced for only a year or two, three years max, then, used up, their commercial usefulness exhausted, they're either put down or—in a poor state like West Virginia—often simply turned loose on the highway to wander until they're rescued.

So you'll sometimes see these classically beautiful dogs racing along with Labs and Shih Tzus and mutts, all teaming up in response to what looks like prey drive, that most basic of instincts. Wendell and Tanya keep a donkey or llama out with their flock of sheep, as these animals will kick at marauding dogs. When most farmers see a pack of dogs who might take it in mind to start running their sheep, they'll likely pick up a rifle, hop in their ATVs, and go out to shoot them.

But what it looks like to us—like a pack of wild dogs taking pleasure in running livestock—may not have predation as its real intent, says dog behaviorist Alexandra Horowitz. This behavior, once adaptive, looks both ancient and atavistic, but it is more likely the more simple autonomic response. When you and I are out on a trail and suddenly break into a run, our dogs will instinctively begin to run with us, keyed in to run when another animal is in motion. So too the dog running after a cat or squirrel: He sees something running and will automatically dash after it, no thought given to what he'd do if he ever caught up to it.

Because greyhounds are bred as racers, they're frequently muzzled to keep them from nipping one another and it may be in the practice of muzzling that they developed the reputation for being biters. Greyhounds are, in fact, not particularly high-strung, and are among the most gentle and physically affectionate of dogs, known for leaning against their owners' legs.

Since they're one of the most ancient breeds, it's a greyhound Odysseus may well have come home to, as Argus is always described as being able to outrun any animal he chases through the woods. The breed has been refined down through the centuries, bred to carry almost no body fat at all and developing the particular nerve-to-muscle ratio that allows their flashes of blurring speed whereby they can burst past a competing dog to win.

Thiebaud was very clearly a sprinter, not built for distances becoming so easily winded. He demonstrated exactly the short-track racer's wound-up, kinetic energy, racing flat out for a brief time, flying around with no thought at all of pacing himself, then collapsing on the rug in a heap.

This was temperamentally so different from Whistler, who'd so loved the long slow trudge along the trails in the Great Cacapon, four or five steady miles being nothing to him.

Our two dogs were proving to be so unlike one another in almost every imaginable way, for which Jack and I were both grateful.

✵ ✵ ✵

On Monday, we drove back to the city with Tee standing on my lap, nose to the glass, as if at attention, staring out at the whole grand world. He acted perplexed, even astonished, that there was all this out there about which he'd had no idea!

And to this day it's his automotive attitude to be on high alert: I have never seen our sight hound so much as blink his eyes on a car trip, no matter how many hours we've been at it, acting as if it's only a fixed co-pilot's gaze that will keep a driver on course.

The little garden apartment we now kept in town was hardly more than a studio, one big room with kitchenette, our bed behind glass doors in an curtained-off alcove. We loved everything about this place, especially its tininess: It was the simple place Jack and I might have had as young people just starting out, had we ever had the chance to be young together and alone in some far-off and romantic city.

Our apartment was on Leroy Place, right on the edge of Dupont Circle in the neighborhood known as Kalorama or Embassy Row. Chuck and Alice Vetter had designed the space when they'd renovated the basement of their hundred-year-old five-story row house.

I hadn't gone in to look with him at apartments because I was up in the country sequestered with my Dark Project. This book was—I then believed—a nonfiction exploration of the effect of suicide on its survivors.

Suicide, like homicide, is simply unlike other deaths in the difficulty of those who remain to make any kind of spiritual sense of it. And the need to try to make sense of it remains an ongoing struggle. I used to think my brothers, our mother, and I were alone in this, but then discovered an astonishing number of people have to deal with these violent ends to their loved ones' lives: For each unexpected death there are an estimated thirty lives, on average, that will be forever altered.

This is the subject area I was given not by the Three Fates, in whom I actually don't much believe, but by their mother, Necessity. Terrible events happen in the lives of so many of us and what a person then does with all this is what remains of interest to me, that we are not passively acted upon by Fate. This belief lies not only at the heart of my work, but in the marrow of my bones where my body produces the blood cells it needs to stay alive. My father's dying as he did didn't make me who I am. Rather, I am what I've become by actively responding to his death—it's in my going on to accomplish what I have that I find true pride and self-worth and even profound happiness.

༄ ༄ ༄

Driving down from the country to town that morning, Jack turned to our new dog to say: Thiebaud, we need to give you a heads-up, all right? Now it's just critically important that you not blow this, got me? Chuck's a pushover, he's so easy he'll be feeding you dog treats from his teeth by this evening, but Alice Vetter just does not suffer fools, so you think you can maybe rein it in?

Our dog was balancing his sharp puppy toenails on my thighs, staring out the windshield intently but he turned to look at Jack like he might be listening, so I went on.

For instance, I told Tee, Alice once confided that—try as she might—she has never liked a Chow. Her sister Mary has a Chow, has always had Chows, but Chows really are sons-of-bitches, if you'll excuse the expression and not to insult your mom, but really— Chows bite people and they bite other dogs and Alice has tried and tried but just can't get herself to like one, so if you have a little Chow tucked away in there, you could maybe keep this to yourself?

I then said to Jack, Alice once told me she has never actually truly loved any dog who was not a Dalmatian.

Do you know what a Dalmatian is? Jack asked Tee. Those black-and-white spotted ones? Maybe we could doctor you up by painting white spots all over you, or if you speak a little Dalmatian, you can maybe fake it?

Our dog, now looking at Jack, smiled and wagged, as if to say: I got this.

And, indeed, as soon as we pulled up in front of the house on

Leroy and saw Alice out in front, bending over her roses, he put his front paws forward on the Pathfinder's dash and started in with this pathetic mewling sound. He sounded plaintive, like he was about to break into sobs, like Jack and I had been keeping Alice from him.

Alice! I called out the rolled-down window. Here's that dog we warned you about. I know he's not exactly Whistler but . . . ?

She looked up from her roses: Thiebaud? she called to him as he stuck his face out the window, still mewling. Well, let him out of the car, she said, and let's see if he'll come to me.

I opened the car door and he was gone, leaping through the air like the dog on the side of the bus flying to get to her, as if—forget Jack and me—it was Alice! he'd been meant for all along.

୪ ୪ ୪

Springtime, the weather fine, cherry blossoms out, Washington's most beautiful season. Jack and I, together in town, would keep the backdoor to our apartment open for Thiebaud so he could wander in and out.

The Vetters' garden was bricked in and his to wander in as he liked. Our dog was keenly aware of all that went on overhead, hearing Chuck and Alice's voices murmuring above us at their kitchen table. Tee would anticipate any Vetter rear guard action by racing outside so he'd be sitting there attentively when their backdoor opened.

Though Thiebaud now seemed to imagine himself to be the Vetters' auxiliary dog, he never scratched to be let in, never barked or even softly woofed. He'd simply sit there patiently, awaiting Chuck, knowing he could count on his man as Chuck was, like Thiebaud himself, a trickster.

Chuck would, for instance, leave the backdoor slightly ajar for Thiebaud, doing this because having that dog in her house so clearly annoyed their dog Jessa, who was now so old she was stiff and crabby.

And because they were in cahoots in their double-teaming of Jessa, Tee quickly learned that when he punched the door with his front paw it might very well swing wide so he could let himself in, and Chuck would be right there, standing tall and patrician by Jessa's cookie jar, saying to his own dog, in all his mock innocence: Well, he let himself in, Jess, you can't blame me if some poor country dog stops in for a cookie.

Jessa turned her nose to one side, as if to avoid having to smell him, then walked away as stiff-legged as a dowager, off to the elevator hallway at the center of the house in order to remove her elegant self from this disreputable company.

Jessa, Alice told us, had never had much of a sense of humor, had always, even as a pup, simply lacked whatever it was that gave Thiebaud his joie de vivre and jolly demeanor. Now in old age—she was nine or ten when we first moved to the Vetters'—Jessa hadn't changed so much as she'd become even more of what she'd always been, a sour and imperious dog used to having all the biscuits in the spotted black-and-white Dalmatian-shaped cookie jar.

And while she tolerated Chuck, she loved Alice to the exclusion of all others and would get up and go to the elevator waiting for someone to help her change floors whenever Chuck invited Thiebaud in. As Jessa hobbled off she'd look at Tee with the pained, facial-muscles-pulled-to-one-side, imperceptibly snarling glare that just has to be the origin of the expression my aunt used to use: getting one's nose out of joint.

Thiebaud never seemed to even notice Jessa's not liking him, but then it wasn't that dog he was interested in, rather he was Argus to Alice's Odysseus, those two the forever-bonded pair.

⚜ ⚜ ⚜

Whenever Thiebaud came inside the Vetters' place he'd tolerate being treated to a biscuit or two from Jessa's cookie jar by Chuck, but would then tear up the stairs in his desperation to find Alice. He needed to find Alice so he could lean against her knees, then grin at Jessa because he'd just come between her and her person.

This behavior—getting between a human and particularly other animals—is called "resource guarding" according to Bob Maida, who clearly did not approve of it. Alice didn't care about either the terminology or what Bob Maida might think—she and Thiebaud just so clearly had their own thing going on, a bond that defied anyone else's understanding. When I had him up in the country with me for more than a few days, she'd call and demand that I bring Tee home to Leroy Place, and from the first she called my dog Mr. Thiebaud.

To this day, Alice is one of Tee's most beloved persons. She says she enjoys visiting with me and Jack when she comes to stay with us in California but it's really her dog Tee that prompts her, at age eighty, to get on a plane and fly three thousand miles to see us.

⚭ ⚭ ⚭

We loved living in the windowless basement of the Vetters' old and elegant house and in the complexly organized and active social life that spun through the formal rooms directly overhead.

Downstairs we were like newlyweds with our half-size range sitting atop a dorm-size fridge, our toaster oven and tiny glass-topped café table, loveseat, two cups and two plates, small TV, great sound system, two short bookcases filled with only a few great books, CDs and DVDs.

And since we very literally could not entertain we'd meet our friends in local restaurants, as do people in France and England and in New York, as it's the truly cosmopolitan person—as Jack and I would tell ourselves—who's happy to live in a microscopic place if this is the price of residing in one of the world's great cities.

The Vetters were wine people, adepts, recipe buffs, true foodists for whom entertaining had become so easy they seemed to have it down to a science. It might be as often as a couple times a week Jack and I, below in our apartment, would begin to hear the incipient noises: the quiet voices of caterers arriving being directed by the soft voice of James, the Vetters' man-of-all-work, china being softly rattled, silver set out, these sounds amplifying until we'd begun hearing the door chimes and bright laughter as guest after guest arrived.

Jack and I are so accustomed to that early-evening bustle going on overhead that one night, as we sit reading and listening to music, we're barely mindful and don't at first notice the abrupt change in the tone of the commotion: a loud slam, then a *bang-boom* coming from the back of the house, this—I'm guessing—might be the caterers moving a piece of furniture?

But then Jack and I simultaneously look up, realizing we do recognize this sound as one we've heard before: It's our landlords' kitchen door being slammed open by some big black insistent dog!

He and I each freeze, and now we're staring at the ceiling as if we can literally see the scene unfolding, so easy to imagine, and it's in dream time that clock logic warps and what's no doubt only seconds seems to transpire over eternity as our half-caste mutt goes greyhounding through the throngs crowding the Vetters' party— almost forty people we later hear—using his double-suspension gallop, wherein his four legs are all fully off the floor, front legs diving through the air, hind legs completely extended backward, then all four paws landing in the same tiny circumference, to be then instantly sprung outward again. A greyhound will automatically race like this, his flexible spine working like a spring to propel the dog forward like he's a foal about to be born.

Even a part greyhound will not canter or trot. Instead he hits the ground running, taking one stride to fly through the kitchen, butler's pantry, dining room, living room, locked on and covering serious ground, veering expertly right or left and so not exactly knocking over this or that astonished guest.

This was, as we'd later hear, a political benefit in which the Vetters were hosting the Bold-Faced Notables but there weren't any major mishaps, in that before Tee got to the front room, he'd caused only a few drinks to slosh and an hors d'oeuvre or two to be dropped, much to Chuck's obvious disappointment, as this was an evening of Inside the Beltway VIPs and Chuck might not have minded seeing this or that Stuffed Shirt upended.

And Chuck would always say he wished he'd had a picture of all those extremely dignified folks poised, mouth open, stopped in mid extremely-important sentence as this huge black dog—who did tend to get bigger each time the story was told—suddenly appeared, tongue lolling, flying between clusters of people, leaping over furniture, bounding over a coffee table laden with canapes and all the lovely cheeses James had set out on Chuck's mother's crystal and china—and here Chuck would be all but choking with laughter as he described the truly astonished expressions of his guests, as room after room fell silent, then the little startled yelps of shock from the folks sitting on the white couches in the alcove in the living room as this dog shows up out of nowhere, leaping into the first lap he sees, this to the far right of the seating group, then rounds the laps of those six seated people like a racetrack, finally arriving at the lap of the one he's sought: Alice, who's in her customary overstuffed white chair.

The party, going from shrieks to completely silent, here paused to decide what it thought of all this, Jack and me then hearing as it explodes into laughter and applause, that, Chuck Vetter, known for being the biggest joker and most relentless tease, had arranged for their evening's pleasure, not some famous singer or cellist or poet of renown, but Thiebaud, the Circus Dog.

⊗ ⊗ ⊗

A few weeks after we get him, Thiebaud and I arrive back in the country having taken the ninety-minute trip from the city and I'm now determined to act and feel and be well enough to stay in this place again, as I need to start back to work on the book I'm writing. I see the message light blinking on the phone on Jack's desk, go to it, and listen to the message.

The next morning we drive together going north along Route 9 to the animal crematorium in Martinsburg, there to collect the wooden box whose brass plaque reads WHISTLER. It's like this that Tee and I together finally bring our poor dog home.

§

the one cake rule

§

Early afternoon, one Sunday in late March. It's the day after Hazel's party when the naked three-year-old T-ballers have romped in Sean and Heida's backyard, an event that's had the odd effect of blessing us, leaving us all in the ebullient mood that makes anything at all seem possible.

We have felt ourselves for the first time to be what we are, that is, a clan, and it's as a family we are now triumphant. We've now realized two miracles achieved by the patchwork of marriage, divorce, remarriage: The first is our nakedly beautiful daughter, niece, cousin, grandchild, Hazel being only the first, we all hope, of many. The second is our One Cake Rule and it goes like this: You have a birthday, you get the one cake, the one party that everyone's invited to.

This is it, we realize, we are learning to get along. Jack calls the expansive feeling we felt that day "This Is Us, Excellent," after the magical story by Mark Richard.

Jack and I are lighthearted because of what we do not yet know: that the future, which is not foretold, will now bear down on us relentlessly. We cannot yet know our dog will die in boarding, that this will prove so traumatic to our mutual psyche that he and I— both separately and together—will be fundamentally changed by it and be all but dislodged from our previously secure surroundings.

For Jack it will confirm his archaic worry that all his dogs die tragically. For me the ancient dream will swirl and coalesce into the same old miasma, becoming the same foggy misery of my broken childhood, which fostered in me a rather grand sense of my own strangeness, the easy sociability that masks a deeper, more profound dis-ease, the feeling that I have no true home, that I belong nowhere and to no one.

Whistler will die in boarding. Our losing him was preventable— had we only known, had we only flown home a single day sooner— and the stuff of this kind of self-recrimination starts in and boringly continues, the blaming, the self-loathing practiced before the court found in the steamy bathroom mirror as when I was getting divorced, and my voice turned shrill and brokenhearted and endlessly repetitive and all there was left to Mike and me was furious disappointment.

Trying to understand how this person you once loved (and somehow still fleetingly do) changed and went a little nuts or else became one day entirely selfish and how the dischord grew until it could no longer be contained and how your Dearest One was changed into the cartoonish person you now secretly call names, somone who now seems like no one you ever really knew, let alone that enchanted person you once stood beside and promised your future to. The Wrong Dog Dream, only so much worse, in that now you awaken to find yourself lying beside exactly the wrong husband.

And how divorce poisons not only the present moment but moves strangely backward in time and outward like oil on water and into the lives of your children and that of your children's children, even as it works to taint the tiny moments that were once so pleasurable, his now hating how much you talk and your becoming increasingly allergic to the chemical scent of his shaving cream.

Whistler's dying as he will seems to break us, change us, will become one of those hinging moments in a life of spiritual catastrophe after which you are never the same again, in that now your path is changed and even that path's meaning.

The Three Fates show up, begin to snip and measure and weave, and suddenly the story of your life is now different and you are now an orphan. These are the moments where we are shown our own velocity, those times when we're flung outward from ourselves and so escape our orbit, in which gravity no longer seems to apply to us, and we begin to outrun our own trajectory. Here come to know our own souls.

In Berkeley Springs, West Virginia, our dog is penned outside that woman's house in his kennel, starving himself and barking. In Berkeley, California, Jack and I are already figuratively packing our thirteen tons of household items—most of this the books that make up the Paradise Library—for our incredible journey back across this whole huge country of ours, we just don't happen to know this yet.

On this day—the Sunday after Hazel's party when Heida and I walk south toward campus on our way to lunch at Liaison—what is honestly momentious is depicted by the tiniest and most incremental things, all subtle, some of it said but much of it not even uttered.

We are part of *Los Compadres*, those of us who share children and grandchildren, those who will make up the kinship system we call the tribe or clan, our being here will soon become even necessary for reasons we cannot yet know.

None of this is yet known, just as none of us knows anything, none of us actually knows the first thing about what's just about to happen, for which I have always been profoundly grateful.

⚘ ⚘ ⚘

Jack and I say grace, at least when we remember. We hold hands across the table, we read from a book called *One Hundred Graces,* or recite the lines of the Buddhist saying that stands framed on our kitchen table: *We venerate the Three Treasures and are thankful for this meal, the work of many people and the sharing of other forms of life.*

This helps us remember to be grateful for the peace we find in that particular instant—the single moment that is at hand—in which we can enjoy being hungry as it heightens the anticipation of being fed just as we're grateful for the moment when we, being tired, can finally crawl into bed.

Grace centers us, helping us remember ourselves as blessed to be alive in this one moment when nothing disasterous is going wrong, at least within the room in which we are just now sitting. Grace organizes us to remember that life is also overwhelmingly composed of the day to day, made up of just such moments at these. It's in our active witness to the ordinary moments that our lives are given meaning, as our dogs are always readily available to tell us.

Jack and I say grace though each of us is either atheist or at least agnostic, neither being able to honestly say he or she believes in God, though I do pray regularly, pray to God right along with our friend Alice Powers and my cousin Carolyn Roll and light the candles I set out on my own private altar, usually asking God for aid concerning a child or a friend or my dog, and this is so often the most simple prayer of all, being the one our friend Annie best expresses as: *Help! Thanks! Wow!*

Both Jack and I were raised in one of the God-the-Father-God-the-Son systems of organized belief, his being one of the American ones where you are self-enabled, in that you consciously choose as a teenager or adult to be baptized into salvation, mine being the one in which your godparents do this for you, as you're christened as a baby wearing—as your father did and your father's father's father—a floor-length white organza christening gown. Each of us is informed by those religious traditions and has the language of the prayers we heard as children not only in our ears and minds but also in our bodies and our souls.

But the true religion of our household is neither Buddhist nor Episcopalian nor American Protestant: It's composed, instead, of the deep faith he and I have in one another. I believe in Jack, believe in what he does, trust him to at least more or less know what he is doing, and Jack, in turn, believes in me.

Jack's belief in me has been absolutely critical, given my orphan's sense of even fundamental shakiness, this even rickety personhood of mine in which I'll feel suddenly cracked by self-doubt, as my basic estimation of myself as writer or wife, mother or friend, teacher, stander-in-line at Trader Joe's, concertgoer, neighbor, dog owner— my existing as any kind of worthy person—starts to feel almost entirely, well, *circumstantial.*

And this is one of the more terrible legacies of my having lost my parents at such a young age.

Jack is simply an optimist by nature, like Thiebaud, like Chuck Vetter, which is so attractive. I have no idea where optimism like this comes from, as Buddhists are so often thoughful practitioners of the most cogent form of spiritual atheism and Jack doesn't believe in the Sky God or much of any kind of God at all. Jack does read the Bible, reads all the holy texts, reads them openmindedly, with both eyes and heart open and not as literature, either, which I take to mean condescendingly. Rather, he reads from within the faith as much as he is able because he believes in faith and is respectful of the work it takes to make a coherent system of belief.

And he has, over the now twenty years he and I have been together, offered the work of his faith as his gift to me.

๛   ๛   ๛

Sometimes you get lucky, sometimes you get the life you actually always wanted, sometimes you look up and find yourself married to this really smart, funny, engaging, and completely competent person your kids call Mr. Dickerson to tease him.

I began this life as an ordinary little girl who was probably, given all that was going on, a little unnaturally cheerful. I wanted only the most ordinary things: to get married and have children. I wanted only to continue to live as I did then walking around in a beautiful world in the company of my dogs and family and friends.

To Be Here Now. To learn to live less in my head and more in this bright world, to feel honestly alive, to be capable of wonder, to truly get that this life is all we can count on, to take it for what it actually is, that is, this everyday miracle. To find the meaningful work you love to do, to work hard enough to get good at it. To eat when you are hungry, to sleep when you are tired, to live as the animals we are by understanding our place in the natural world, then becoming respectful enough as to take up less room in it.

To be less the person I've been—lost and wounded and aggrieved —and more like my friend Alice Vetter, who doesn't have time for that, who was put in a camp by the government of her own country, whose family, consigned to Idaho, lost its place in California. Alice, who while in that camp contracted TB, who has diabetes and is a survivor of cancer, and whose fat, old dog Jessa died just a few short months after Alice lost Chuck, her husband of more than fifty years.

Alice was so torn up by the death of Jessa that people were mad at her, saying she wasn't in her right mind when she went out and immediately found her own Replacement Dog—my own Mr. Thiebaud, as she explained it—who was this almost astonishingly ugly rescued Boston terrier named Chooey, who seemed so strange-looking to me as to be almost repellent, and was named Chooey, evidently, because he did, in fact, chew up everything: couches, draperies, pillows, bottle caps, corks, aluminum cans, electrical cords, but Alice— relentlessly, even defiantly—loved that dog anyway.

You know you act more wounded over the death of that nasty worm of a Dalmatian than you ever did over Dad, one of her kids said to Alice.

They're free to think whatever they want to think, Alice said, as she was telling me this story. They cannot judge me, as they honestly have no idea of what is actually in my heart.

I do, Alice: I know it's not that we love our animals more than we do our people, only that our feelings about our people are complicated so it's only in the loss of an animal we feel this honest and pristine, as if there is nothing in our lives that has ever been more true.

⚮ ⚮ ⚮

That fine spring weekend Heida and I are walking down Shattuck to have lunch at a certain bistro. She is tall and blonde and dignified. Each of us has the same long-in-this-country Dutch ancestry, each the California desert-rat painter grandmother, and each of us was born in Alta Bates, in the same hospital in which she and I will, eventually, have had all our babies and this puts us all up there together on what's known as "The Cradle Roll."

Heida and I are fond of one another, but could hardly be tempermentally more different.

She and Sean have been together since they were teenagers—I've now known them almost as long as I've known Jack so I know Heida to be in no way a changeling, in that she's always been much as she is now, a self-possessed young woman. She works as an art conservator, hired by museums and private collectors to restore photos and works on paper, a job that perfectly suits her, as this work requires her to be what she already so naturally is, which is painstaking and methodical, diligent and calm.

This gorgeous day! Sunshine so clean, air so lightly fragrant with citrus, you understand why they've founded this world-class institution of higher learning exactly here, directly opposite the Golden Gate, why they named the streets Euclid and Bancroft and Hearst, all resonant with bold curiosity and the Westward feeling of all our expansive hope.

Heida lives with Sean in the house she herself grew up in and we're walking from their house in the direction of campus, down a street she's walked maybe a thousand times.

She and Sean are the rock at the heart of our family, upon which we have built this matrix. They stand as these tall lean people at its center and lend the rest of us their stability, which is odd to me, feeling like it should have been the other way around, and might have been had Jack's and my generation not had the small problem we seemed to have had called divorce.

In that we all got divorced, we divorced, then we remarried, sometimes several times, and it's through this particular weave that our granddaughter Hazel gets her complex network of stepaunts and stepuncles, stepcousins and whole passel of grandparents.

It was during the time that Heida was in Delaware at Winterthur, doing her graduate work in art conservancy, that she and Sean, there in the East with her, decided to get married. They were married in the Brazil Room in Tilden Park by Robert Aitken, author of *Taking the Path of Zen*. Aitken Roshi has been Jack's teacher for the past thirty-five years.

The grandparental group erected around Sean and Heida's wedding stood over them like a chuppah and was then cemented in place by the birth of Hazel. We're the Clan, *Los Compas*, and we are as good at the work of getting along as we were maybe terrible at being married to the people were were originially married to.

Not only that, we enjoy it. We're like a real family, we gossip and look askance but we also understand how necessary we are to our mutual well-being and so we work well together.

And this alone is its own triumph, so in times of celebration too we raise a glass looking down the long holiday table, saying *Viva nosotros! viva los Compas!* Here's to us! with real love and affection.

ॐ ॐ ॐ

A family, as it evolved, as it grew and is growing still in the same manner as a coral reef, an open-ended system that is welcoming by style and always being amended.

The human kinship system has needed to be adaptive in order to be successful, and no one can argue with our ability to dominate an environment, despite our myriad beastly weaknesses. We are made most extraordinarily vulnerable by the fact that our young take so long to reach an independent maturity. In an industrialized society it's easy to spend the better part of the three decades absorbed in this task.

And it's because of the necessity of all these fragile bonds of inter-connectedness we've evolved the entire apparatus of culture upon which we predicate households and towns, nations and empires in which we invest all the power and beauty of creation myth. It is human culture that allows us to tell our stories back to ourselves, as we are those animals ever in need of the explanations offered by stories telling us who we are and where we're from and where we think we might be going. In this way, art and literature and history and science and religion all contribute to our shared myth of origin.

One of the great evolutionary advances for the dog is his capacity to step into the domesiticated scene and be flexible in his role, alpha in one situation, beta the next. This is why the dog could be brought into our familial network when the lion or the wolf cannot.

And what we've done as a family is work at the job of working together, not because this is easy or because we're exemplary people but because we are the ones who made the gigantic costly societal mess—and mess is exactly what a divorce is, at least when children are involved.

So in this clan of ours we both cleave and cleave. We came apart long ago and didn't like the lonely feeling, so now we stick tightly together.

᙮ ᙮ ᙮

As soon as Heida and I are seated in the café, the question arises: Are you and Jack at least talking about moving home? she asks.

We are always talking about it, I say. But it's all so complicated, with Eva still in school in the East and I'm teaching now, at long last, and we've made such close friends and . . . ?

It isn't really Jack, I go on. Really, Heida, he'd be back here in a minute. The problem is me. The problem's that same thing I've always had that I've told you about, you know, with the power of memory?

In truth I have what's called an eidetic memory for all the minutiae of disaster. This is, no doubt, a coping mechanism developed in response to all that early personal trauma. I'm like a war correspondent, I get steely, cold, totally rational. I see and hear and comprehend everything really clearly, committing all of it to 3-D memory, so it's stored in the haptic place you can go to and enter, but because it's traumatic it's not a memory palace, more like levels of Dante's hell.

But what's terrible about this is that I'm plagued with double vision, whereby I can be peacefully driving down the streets and roads of the town where I was born, and turn a corner, and abruptly discover myself utterly transported into that other narrative. I don't remember these things, I reexperience them in excruciating detail, it's like I've left that highway and have driven down the lane into that thick dense past, one pulsing with my haunted sense of emptiness.

But when you come home, Heida says to me, you'll be making new memories. Everything new will be actually happening, all these new things that are really occurring every single day.

And this moves me profoundly, as Heida and Sean are our stern children, such a tight and efficient unit and so reticent with their feelings that you're never exactly sure that they—well?—even really like you.

I am so moved but don't want to break down and openly weep, which would embarrass both of us, so I say my usual flip and deflective thing: So's what's the word on the homefront? Any banner news?

Which is code between us for what isn't not said, for magical reasons, that she and Sean are trying, again, to get pregnant, and we don't speak of it because, for them, the matter of getting pregnant and staying pregnant has not been easy.

Come to think of it, Heida says, I'm maybe feeling something? tired? headachy? sore breasts? Probably just getting my period.

Tired? I think. Sore breasts? And I now take a good long look at my daughter-in-law who is seated directly opposite me two and a half feet away and I see what is just glaringly apparent: that Heida's changed, that she looks different from the way she looked even yesterday, that her face is mottled in a bright hormonal patchwork. But it's more than this, there is a different aspect to her physical person that exudes radiance. It's like the light around her entire being has changed, as if the world itself is softening, drawing in all its sharp and glinty angles.

Know what? I say, lifting my water glass to clink with hers, I am often a little witchy about these things and I'll betcha anything I am looking at a pregnant girl.

It's about a month or so later Sean emails his dad, subject line reading: Yup!

Uh-oh, Jack emails back. There goes the TV room.

More like Uh-oh, Uh-oh, Sean replies, which is when Jack picks up the phone.

Twins? really? I am blown down by this news. I found the work of having just one baby at a time so completely exhausting it was hard for me to get my mind around how anyone might manage twins. How, for instance, were you expected to get them safely across the street?

Marcel and Katrina were born at Alta Bates in November of 2004. Jack flew home to be there and has not—so far—missed the birth of any of his grandchildren.

Then a little more than a month later, he, Eva, Thiebaud, and I flew home to Berkeley for Christmas. It takes Mr. Dickerson, our lawyer, to talk our dog in his crate onto this nonstop flight, as we'll not be boarding *this* dog, thanks.

We stayed, as we customarily do, at the Golden Bear Motel on San Pablo at Cedar, right across the street from Alice Water's Café Fanny, where you have Berkeley in confluence, this little city of a hundred thousand in haiku: the high culture of the best food you can imagine exactly across the street from a very nice and clean motel where whores and their pimps argue loudly in the parking lot. We not only like this motel, this is what we like about this motel, as it tends to remind you that for most people on this earth life is not My How and Why Wonder Book.

The Golden Bear Motel will make you feel like you're in a reasonable city, somewhere less like America and more like Amsterdam. And then there's this about it: The Golden Bear's the only lodging in Berkeley where you can have your dog.

Sean and Heida live in a two-story brown shingled craftsman on the flats, a house that once seemed spacious, even big for just the two of them. This same house now seems completely overwhelmed. And these two are our tidy, very well-organized kids, who not only have a lot of stuff, but also take good care of their stuff—at least they used to.

Now it seems there is no more room in this house for anything. It isn't the two burrito-shaped, small, very portable packages that are the new babies, exactly, but all the equipment that seems to have been delivered in an oversize moving van, also the Christmas tree, stockings, the gifts, the relatives who've arrived to bring these gifts.

Their usually tidy house now looks even end-of-the-worldish, like a beach after the last great storm, strewn with all this errant human debris.

⚜ ⚜ ⚜

A dark and rainy winter, blinds drawn against the cold, cats-without-names mewling out there in the chill, a clot of opened umbrellas blocking the front door, dripping coats in the foyer, rooms too small to hold this legion of well-intentioned Loved Ones, lights dimmed by rheostat, pockets of quiet chatter, muffled noises from the kitchen, then somewhere off there somewhere someone is crying inconsolably, screams or wracking sobs.

And no one's on top of the necessary fix-its: that half the overhead lights in the dining room are burned out, that cups and dishes sit everywhere, that someone—and not particularly helpfully—has swooped by to make the way-too-elaborate brunch.

What is maybe most surprising is that these are our eldest, our most together kids, and that they've been defeated as surely as every foreign power has been in trying to invade Afganistan.

It's perhaps the level of defeat that's shocking, given that Sean and Heida came amply equipped with what kids need starting out: a long relationship, jobs, house, the maybe even overabundance of grandparental backup, that we are this complex matrix of the active, the willing, the emotionally involved, this phalanx of creative thinkers, who start as an orderly formation that then tends to overrun this house like a high-achieving horde.

Jesus! and to think that we are this highly trained and synchronized batallion with all these accomplishments and graduate degrees and the work of caring for two newborn human infants can still completely defeat us?

Which is maybe what the human family is, that given adequate food supplies we become so successful as to expand and overfill whatever place we're at, and must, therefore, set out for the new place we seem to need to colonize? That we are this clan, that we have formed this large family, that there are so many of us has itself become the problem.

Christmas arrives. More of *Los Compas* show up. It's the holidays. People want, naturally enough, to eat something. These food events are positioned at more or less appropriate intervals throughout the day, morning, noon, and evening, as the strategically placed food event is more or less what this clan of ours is good at. And these food events must now always take place at the house of Sean and Heida as their three children, who—taken together!—weigh less than forty-nine pounds, are holding the rest of our entire operation hostage.

So, in entering into the house on Bonita, you come by stealth, hoping no one will notice. You try to be small and quiet and voice no opinion. You want to seem as invisible as the brownies in the fairy stories, who will do good deeds in the night then vanish.

What would actually help our kids most, of course, is for everyone to leave and to do that exactly now. All that's standing between us and everyone's leaving is this one final food event that we all must just necessarily get through.

This last food event has been ordered by phone and Jack and Demian are the lucky ones as they get to leave here at least for some portion of an hour to drive to pick it up.

Suzanne—who is Demian's new bride—and Eva and I are, as quietly as possible, putting the leaves into the dining table working in the twilight of the overhead burned-out fixture. This is to be the most no-fuss Christmas Eve dinner anyone can imagine, that is, the Jewish one, which is Chinese takeout, which seems appropriate since many in our clan are in one way or another at least somewhat Jewish.

What dinner will consist of is countless white boxes of that unnaturally bright green and radioactively orange, very shiny takeout, all of it tainted with MSG and designated by random kanji written in black felt-tip marker and there are massive amounts of all of it as Jack has immodestly ordered two or three of everything, just to be sure, of what no one's exactly certain.

Eva and Suzanne and I are working silently, communicating by our ad hoc ASL, ordering Shem and Noah by gesture to gather chairs, getting out silver, glasses, spreading the largest tablecloth, which isn't big enough and we've just about finished. We aren't speaking as we're mindful that Mom, as they'll call you in the Breastfeeding Circumstance, is right overhead nursing one baby or maybe—though terrible to think about—two, when suddenly something appears on the stairs there as suddenly as an apparition in one of those Japanese horror films, if there were tall blonde ghosts in Japanese horror films:

It's the body of my calm daughter-in-law Heida except she's been possessed.

No! whatever spirit that took Heida screams. No tablecloth! Someone will have to wash it! No cloth napkins! Use the paper ones they give you! No knives! No forks! What do you think they give you *chopsticks* for?

And Sean, who is standing in his tall way in the kitchen doorway, arms long, fists clenched against either thigh, says to me, Next year, through lips that do not move.

They learned this in their Multiples' Support Group: All you must do is survive Year One, as Sean has told us. You survive Year One in order to get to Year Two.

Next year, Sean and Heida are currently promising one another. We'll make real food next year, go for a walk next year, we'll read a book next year, put leaves in the table and spread a tablecloth, polish silver, light a fire in the fireplace, next year.

We will celebrate Christmas next year.

There was almost never a time during Year One, Sean later told his dad, that someone in their household was not falling asleep just as someone else was waking up. The jumbled, psychotic cycles of sleeping and waking of the two new babies and Hazel turning four made it hard for them to ever predictably go much of anywhere, so they stayed in that dark house.

And the twins were fraternal, a boy, a girl, and developmentally very different, so they never formed the tidy, well-organized duality they'd hear other parents (who are liars) bragging about in their twins group. Marcel learned to crawl months before Katrina, who kept up with her brother through the sheer force of will, also, frankly, by using him as a tool. Marcel would crawl to get some toy out of her reach, and she'd lean over to grab him by the diaper, haul his body back, take the toy away from him.

Marcel had huge brown eyes. He'd look up, shocked, as if to say, No fair!

Next year, Sean and Heida promised one another, everyone will sleep through the night, we'll go on a vacation trip next year!

I'd been reading up on the way of the macroorganism, how coral reefs are colonies made of a compendium of individuals all interdependently organized, how the single polyp will secrete a carbonate exoskeleton that adheres to make the house, how corals grow best in warm, shallow, and sunny water.

Our family was like this, I realized, a matrix of complex interconnectednesses in which Jack and I needed to be in close proximity in order to participate. He and I had begun to imperceptibly turn west, as a plant will turn, to follow the setting sun.

The week after Christmas we flew East and began making arrangements. Amazingly, it was our oldest and most self-sufficient kids who needed us, and we were moving home.

3

wonder years

We are lonesome animals. We spend all our
life trying to be less lonesome. And one of the
ancient methods is to tell a story.

JOHN STEINBECK

no place like 127.0.0.1

But why would Jack and Jane move to Emeryville? their friends and family wondered, considering who they were and where they'd been and how much stuff they had, and understanding—as everyone must—that this place was maybe a little bit of a toy town still? in that it's only now discovering what it might grow up to be?

Was it only that Emeryville had nothing posttraumatic about it? That it lay outside the blast-zone of Eidetic Memory, all those Bull's-eyes and Radiating Spheres of Failure and Defeat, that it wasn't Lake Merritt where my mom used to lock herself out of her apartment when I was working at Cal and I'd have to ride my bike from campus—ten miles there, ten back on my lunch break—to help her get back in?

That it wasn't the Elmwood, where I'd lived as a young person, that it wasn't the Rockridge, where Mike and I had married and had our babies, that it wasn't the Northside hills for Jack, as that's where he and Victoria split up, or the Northside flats for the two of us together, where we sold the huge three-story house he and I once owned for some measly pittance in the minor real estate slump right before that whole rocket ship took off so that house now stands like this giant architectural monument to our profound financial incompetence?

Why would we choose Emeryville? Because his publishing offices were right there and we were being practical, for once? Because we'd read that a household could save about ten thousand dollars a year by giving up one car, so we guessed we'd move to this *completely automotively dependent state!*—for this is surely what California is—and give this latest of our Grand Unified Theories a whirl?

But more simply it was probably this: Because Emeryville was somewhere neither Jack nor I had ever lived, it had neither good nor bad associations for us and retained, therefore, an aura of fictional possibility.

Many of the places I've never lived reach out to me with this allure, as if you can enter there into the otherworldly, which has that particularly bright and gauzy texture, the same hopeful feeling of light and air lifting the curtain of an open window. It beckons to you, as if the future there isn't set, that it's still loose, even hypothetical, so you feel as if you can participate in this future, as if a million beautiful things may still happen to you.

༄ ༄ ༄

Emeryville, California: once famous for its light industry, the bakeries and coffee roasters and commercial laundries that supplied San Francisco's grand hotels. It also had the seedy underside that seems to appeal to Jack and me, the gaming rooms, brothels, racetrack, now going, going, gone as this little city yups itself up and enters into twenty-first-century respectability.

Its main street is named Hollis, after the mayor who managed to stay in office for more than forty years running on the platform of his town's resolute and profound godlessness: Come to E'ville, the saying went, to drink and whore and gamble, Mayor Hollis pledging to keep all churches out of his booming little sin-filled town.

True to his word, whenever a church would try to sneak in by establishing itself in one of the anonymous storefronts along San Pablo Avenue, he'd do nothing to oppose it, just call a city council meeting to redraw the boundaries, simply shunting off that offending block into either Berkeley or Oakland.

Emeryville is now a hippish place of five or seven or even eleven thousand, numbers so much in flux that every population sign says something v*astly* different. Home to Pixar Studios and you can maybe best witness a somewhat skewed portrait of E'ville outside the factory in *Monsters, Inc.*, a postmodern-ish, cartoonishly futuristic place, an adhocracy, sort of adolescently perverse.

Also home to Rudy's Can't Fail Café, owned by members of the rock band Green Day, with its long shelves in the back room lined with dozens of plex-cased monsterized and zombied and tricked-out whorish Barbies, where you can order an alcoholic milkshake. Here the gourmet mac and four-kinds-of-cheese is brought to you by hipster servers with spiked-up dyed black hair, great stone-hard bodies, blasted full-sleeve tats, and those facial piercings done in such truly inventive ways that these would honestly have never occurred to you.

And because I tend to fall into sympathetic resonance with my surroundings I am immediately pursuaded by the playground spirit of a place like this and buy a Rudy's tee shirt and I—feeling all stylish and inspired—then take it directly home and attempt to cut it up, which—as I then immediately discover—is actually a really hard thing to artistically do.

Emeryville: the kind of place where highly successful grown-up children go to live out their Wonder Years, and this is an actual stage in the healthy person's psychological development, one most of us simply pass through without getting stuck. The Wonder Years is what you leave when you're suddenly dumped into the gloom of adolescence, when you discover you are neither going to be able to fly or turn invisible, that your dog *will* die, your parents suck, and *déjà vu* means no past lives currently being revisited, you've just been riding in the backseat of the car too long.

The Wonder Years is that time when you are still capable of what is clinically known as "magical thinking," when you enjoy the act of simply *pretending*, when all is still haloed by the glow of play, when you still *honestly believe* you can become anything you like— astronaut, spokesmodel, billionaire philanthropist, novelist—as nothing has happened to yet dissuade you.

      ❦ ❦ ❦

Our new apartment complex in Emeryville is both new and truly complex, brand new, in fact, in that it wasn't finished when we signed the lease, the two of us choosing this place in another of what are whispered about by our Loved Ones as what might be politely called another of Jack and Jane's *residential whims*.

Truly, Jack and I have long had this larky, kind of pin-the-tail-on-the-donkey habit of choosing the venue in which we guess we'll just flounce off and conduct the next portion of our lives. Morgan County was another of those impulses that just seemed *to play out,* where we guessed we'd just go live for a while in yet another of these rather *unlikely* places, as if we imagine ourselves to be characters in someone's cracked version of a life, like it's one of those zany Lucy and Desi–type roadtrips.

We picked the apartment in Emeryville sight unseen in a blurry drive-by on a December night, with wind and rain storming in off the Pacific with such force it was raining sideways. We were out in one of those miniscule white rental cars that seem to be designed for tiny Filipina grandmothers that was now carrying four full-size adults, plus all of D and Suzanne's luggage, as well as a huge, wet eighty-five-pound black tagalong who needed to stand up in the backseat because he knew he was *really* a Shetland pony. We'd been driving around in the rain for a while, having checked out of our motel and on our way to offload D and Suz and their luggage at the airport when Suzanne, who has extremely high executive function, thought to call to discover that their flight from OAK to SEA-TAC had been massively weather-delayed so we now had even more horrible hours to kill and nowhere to go because you cannot leave a Shetland pony in a rental car when he's afraid of thunderstorms.

Hours to kill, nowhere to go, in that we'd already said good-bye to our Loved Ones and we had our dog with us, which made us completely unwelcome in the homes of our cat-loving Loved Ones and anyway who wants to go back and endure another holiday food event once you've finally put *all that* behind you?

So we were out bungling around in this terrible weather, me and Suz in the back of the car with this enormous wet dog standing in our laps, her asking me, Does he ever just relax and sit down? and me saying, Nope, and her saying, Why? and me saying, I have no idea, maybe he thinks he might miss something?

And it's right about there we happen by the truly horribly ugly black-glass building housing Jack's publishing's company's California offices and notice the FOR LEASE sign in the window of the leasing office directly across the street.

Jack parked, he and D got out. Suzanne and me barely noticing as were were by then deeply in conversation behind our own personal wet black dog apparatus, talking about what you'd call a tiny Filipina grandmother, then grandmother names in general, and what her mom—whose family's from Sicily—would preferred to be called when Suzanne and Demian had kids and it was then I discovered that my own grandma name, which is Nonni, happens to mean *several* Italian grandmothers.

Hey, Tee, Jack said, as he slid back into the toy car's driver's seat, you're in luck. This place has a liberal pet policy. There was rain beading on the lenses of his glasses and dripping from his hooded jacket all down his face, which might have looked like tears except that he was grinning.

Great, I said. Let's do it.

Do what? Suz said.

Move here, I said.

Move here? Suzanne asked me, now looking profoundly shocked.

Well, I said, why not? They take dogs, which means we won't have to try to sell You Know Who on eBay, because, let's face it, no one but Alice Vetter would spend one nickle buying him, no offense, Thiebaud. And you'd be *simply amazed* by all the mindless prejudice there is out there in the rental-leasing world against any dog with any kind of meat on his bones. Most places won't allow you any dog who weighs more than a teacup poodle.

There's going to be a lap pool, D added.

A lap pool? I said. See? *All meant to be!* Sign us up.

Sign you up? My daughter-in-law was now openly staring at me.

Sure, I said. It's convenient and it looks nice.

It doesn't *look nice,* Jane, she said. It *looks like* a construction site. You cannot be serious?

I smiled at Suz, my blithe little Mona Lisa smile. Suzanne was then still new to our family and so *had no idea* of the rash housing things Jack and I have gone and together done.

ଙ ଙ ଙ

The digital—as I am discovering by my constant hanging out at the new Apple store on "Bay Street," where there didn't use to be such a thing as "Bay Street"—is only another sort of sort, the Yes, the No, the one, the zero. The digital is not my enemy and it doesn't have it in for me, nor was it specifically created in order to either shame me or make me feel clumsy.

Instead the digital is the name for a new Bay Street–ish type landscape, which is simply a topographical abstraction that lies as transparent overlay on the land in which I was born. Unlike my children, I am not a digital native and grew up in a more dog-walking place, the hills and dales and creeks and inlets that have been known for the past ten thousand years as "Shellmound."

This is a statement of fact, not a judgement. The analog is merely the name given the geography into which I was born, where the more land-based person such as I is more used to getting most of her information. It is the analog world that the dogwalker trudges in which we go up and down conforming to gravity and over and around its more solidly three-dimensional hills.

When we left Berkeley in the midnineties to move to Washington, Jack and I had a fax machine, but I didn't yet use email. I had an email account, as was required of me in that I was teaching at Davis, but I also had a TA whose job it was to read those emails and to tell me—as tactfully as possible—what they seemed to want to say. I was excused from reading my own emails because email was too upsetting. It was then too upsetting and still often is particularly to the kind of person I am, which is someone so sensitive to language this borders on the phobic.

And now here Jack and I are—after a decade away in Washington—plopped right back down here in Emeryville, where Jack's business is housed in a black glass building called EmeryTech, which looks like a miniature Century City made, perhaps, of black glass Legos and resembling in no way a building that might house a literary publishing house.

EmeryTech is also home to the so-called campus of an entity called Silicon Valley College, or SVC, in which all teaching and all learning takes place online. People come and go in silence from what appears to be a clean room, in which there are no teachers. Tests are given, certifications issued. No one in the rest of Jack's building has the slightest idea what it is that's being studied there, or what this otherworldly realm of knowledge might even begin to pertain to.

These people earn a diploma reading SILICON VALLEY COLLEGE. In the physical sense of where we are geographically located—the stone-aged locale known to Ohlone People as "Shellmound"—we are at least fifty crow-flying miles from anything like the analog pin-drop that renders a *real* Silicon Valley, which is actually *light years away*, with traffic.

Many of the people in our apartment building seem to be this kind of Clean-Room, nonanalog, Design-Within-Reach, toy-dog, rented-plant type Tiny Person, about to spend a cartoon instant in this little toy town, wearing shirts and caps on which the words LIFE IS GOOD have been embroidered in slave-wage sweatshops in the PRC, then brought here via container ship.

They speak, therefore, of what's in their *wheelhouse,* their current *occupational tool kit,* and, FYI, there are such things now as *takeaways,* what's on their SVC CV and it's these fucking TLAs anymore that I'm obviously supposed to be up on and this place full-on reeks of new carpet made of fossil fuels so every step I take sends up ancient animal screams and there's a weird techy vibe to the complexity of this complex where Jack and I now evidently live, which is set almost *exactly* atop the place we used to live, which—as I look around—seems to be here no more.

We are only 2.3 miles, seven minutes by car, with traffic, an easy hike, from the hospital in which I was born, so I am only a stone's throw, figuratively speaking, from Alta Bates where I took my literal first breath but I keep experiencing the strange Time-Space parallax Pacific Islanders call *paling,* which is nothing more than failing to recognize—in the most profound and spiritual sense—a place you ought to know.

My husband, who's an Early Adopter and Techno-Forward, will explain my out-of-body thing—when it becomes apparent to those around us—by saying, She cannot really be communicated to in this language—and here Jack'll drop his voice confidentially to let you know you're in on the joke—because, as you know, *Miss Vandenburgh is from Spain.*

Miss Vandenburgh is from Spain is a far-too-complicated-to-be-told-here joke between my husband and me that references my writerly ability to simply dream myself sideways and off the grid of wherever I *really* am and go psychologically MIA. I just *get gone*, as if I am physically proceding down an entirely different narrative byway. *Miss Vandenburgh is from Spain* references a writer's true ability to shape-shift, change instantly to Spirit Animal, then vanish behind the fictional curtain into an Entirely Different Realm.

Jack, the Buddhist, tells me, *Be Here Now*, an age-old adage used by one of those New-Aged Gurus back in the Olden Days. *Be Here Now* is a sentiment with which I'm in profound sympathy as it speaks of Shellmound, that is, basic human need to just go squat together on the flat rock and crack open a few more oysters, accomplishing *nothing* more important than sustenance, which is what sustains us and keeps us going: a little talk, some food, being physically close to your Birthday Friends who do not speak to you in the latest Three Letter Acronym to display their hipnitude but feel entirely comfortable laying the skin of their bare arm lightly against the skin of your bare arm and nothing's meant by this so there's no need for anyone to get creeped out.

And what has any of this accomplished? We've just tossed a few more shells up on the shellmound of posterity, which is why all the snotty Big Shot anthropologists demean this beautiful place of ours and our Indians as Belly Culture Ones, just because we never come up with much more technologically advanced than sharpened sticks and pretty baskets.

And our apartment complex actually is complex, in that it has a West Side and an East Side that are just enough alike to completely fool a person as digital as my husband, so Jack has, on several occasions, become so completely lost in these complexities he's had to call me on his cell phone so Miss Vandenburgh, from Spain, can verbally walk him home again.

Jack got the name The Pathfinder—and this is what he's called by our kids—through his habit of getting exceptionally lost. He's not only lost, he belongs to that class of individual known as "Lost, with Control Issues," for whom confusion causes anger and defiance rather than calm Buddhistic acceptance of the existential truth of one's own lostness, so when Jack's lost he tends to become even more stubbornly lost, as he feels the need to illogically argue with anyone trying to help him.

His becoming belligerently lost was one of the reasons he and I almost got divorced on our Incredible Journey driving the nearly three thousand miles back across this country, also why we almost never got married in the first place. Jack and I were out looking at places where two nice people might get married when he became so bitterly entrenched in his defiance of his terminal lostness I realized I'd need to leap from the car in order to break the spell and hopped out barefoot onto Georgia Avenue, as I recall, taking with me only a handful of parking change.

Now, with him on the phone, I must walk Jack from The Pool Side of the Complex where he's been tricked into wandering by its wrong-way-mirror-like parallax, to The Dog Side where The Pathfinder lives with Miss Vandenburgh, his Spanish Bride, also the eighty-five-pound West Virginia porch hound named Wayne Thiebaud, who more and more in these close quarters seems to resemble a Shetland pony.

Into the cramped rooms of this pretty small apartment are also crammed thousands of The Pathfinder's zillions of things, many of which—and this is *increasingly disturbing* to his bride—seem to have WORDS on them. The man has, for instance, *dozens* of coffee mugs all with words on them, words referencing places visited or causes ascribed to or bought because certain phrases—STAMP OUT

TYPE ABUSE!—once struck somone as funny? He also has dozens of similarly languaged tee shirts, also all kinds of fan gear, for the SF Giants, Cal Bears Boosterisms, and for the Forty-Niners, all these jackets and caps and rally flags, as well as banners that decree his ongoing allegiance to the Baltimore Orioles, also bird books and cookbooks and plant books and flower books and star books, as well as stacks and stacks of magazines, many of which seem to have to do with *nature*, and *Christ,* as his bride's mother used to say, *do I hate nature.*

This man, as Miss Vandenburgh is shocked to realize, has in his possession literally *thousands and thousands of typographically significant objects,* and this is *not counting* the books in the man's library, as books will in no way fit in this smallish newish place of theirs and so are being currently housed, in neatly stacked boxes that weigh more than twenty-seven thousand pounds—and I must pause here so this number may be reemphasized, as it is *THIRTEEN TONS!*—right down the street and across the railroad tracks from the E'ville complexity at the Five Star Rent-A-Space so the Organized Hoarder and his Shetland can at least nod in the direction of the Paradise Library as they trot calmly by.

There is something *just so deeply wrong,* Miss Vandenburgh thinks, with this new chapter of their once-promising life story, in that it's just *wrong* for these people to be living in a cramped and too-small place where there's nothing to read except *tee shirts* and *coffee mugs!* and for this man to be not only lost but so *entrenched in his own lostness* that he can't see what he's become, which is perhaps the most materialistic Buddhist ever known in the history of recorded time.

ও ও ও

My dog and I have had it with E'ville and the unpleasant changes it seems to have wrought in us, his turning pony, and my seeming to have become some variety of out-of-place Pacific Islander, and so we spend much of our days walking the halls in the magical belief that we're walking back across the country.

We keep track of the miles we're trekking on our pedometer as we map the complexities of these buildings the old-fashioned way, hallway after hallway, all virtually identical, with almost nothing interesting to see. He and I walk along, my dog heeling along obediently past all the silent metal doors, past doors of all these untutored dogs, who snarl and scratch and growl and woof on the other side and my dog is hurt that dogs on this side of the world would feel free to act like this.

As Thiebaud and I walk along we're reading the various doormats that folks have left out in order to distinguish themselves. Hazel, now four, will walk along with us while visiting and has recently told me we have the prettiest doormat of them all. What she actually said was this: Nonni, you and Jack have the prettiest doormat in your whole hotel.

Hazel believes we live in a hotel because, while she's stayed in hotels, she has no previous experience with any person actually living in a place like this, many stories high, with East Sides, West Sides, Street Sides, Train Sides, and huge banks of elevators and the long anonymous hallways where her grandfather is sometimes so hopelessly lost she and I have needed to saddle up our sight hound and form the posse deputized to go search for him.

Many of the doormats reference the animal occupant, we've notice. One doormat down the way has a message from a captured cat, I read aloud: "Day 73. My Captors continue to torture me with the feathered object . . ."

What does that mean? Hazel asked.

It's a joke, I said.

A few hallways later she said, Why's it funny?

Hazel, I said, I have no idea.

My dog and Hazel and I are clocking these expeditions on my pedometer as we're walking our way back where we've recently come from, which is 2322 Leroy Avenue, Washington, DC, 20018, and where I've left all my Birthday Friends. So far we've clocked nearly a hundred miles, which means we only have about 2,700 to go. When I hit the PED icon on my phone to give me the time in days it reads:

WALKING DIRECTIONS BETWEEN THESE LOCATIONS CANNOT BE FOUND.

In our travels Thiebaud and I one day notice that the cat doormat has been moved four doors down the hall to an apartment where no cat—as we happen to know—resides. This indicates that the new apartment is this cat's off gravity, or digital, address.

The mat's been moved because the cat's analog apartment has a new doormat that reads: There's No Place like 127.0.0.1. I know all about where this cat does and does not reside because I've met the people who own this cat: SJ, whose initials stand for Sara Jane—she's from Nottingham and lives with a man named Han, for Han Solo.

Han and SJ are BPs, she says. And because she's maybe worried that I might be too analog to get it, SJ then adds: BP stands for Bed Partners.

I nod, I smile my new smile, which I'm calling Wise Virgin.

Got it, I say, neutrally, and then SJ then goes on for a while about how she and Han were, in fact, married a few months back in the forest near Tahoe that had been done up by their friends to look like Arden. Each wore a green tunic and emerald leggings and little elfin shoes with bells on their upturned toes, and had their hair professionally dyed distinctively matched shades of reddish-streaky-tawny that each still sports, but none of this, they've found, makes them feel that different from how they felt before, that is, they don't yet feel exactly married?

Well, the Wise Virgin says, these things take time.

SJ nods gravely, and I'm guessing she and I are maybe onto something, so I'm encouraged to go on:

It's a process, I continue. You get married but that doesn't exactly do it. It's more like you wake up one day thinking, oh, so this is what it's like to be married.

SJ's presses her lips together, thinking this over, then asks, out of nowhere, Do you like magic?

Yes, I say, but I am lying. I do not, in fact, like magic. Or rather, I do like magic, real alchemical magick, the transformative kind they spelled with a *k* in the Olden Days, but I don't really care for magicians. I don't like magicians because I don't believe in them, I even resent magicians in that they prey on believers, my husband, being credulous, is one of them.

Actually, I say to SJ, it's my husband who likes magicians.

Have you read the Harry Potters? she asks.

Yes, I say, lying. I haven't read a single word of even one of the Harry Potters, don't even know their titles, but I also haven't spoken to another living soul—aside from my dog and my husband and my favorite four-year-old—for at least a couple of days, so I seem to want to continue having this conversation.

But I feel neither the need to read a Potter, nor to tell Sara Jane the truth of this, as it's my own little secret, just as I felt no compelling need to know one more single fucking thing more about the life of Benjamin Franklin than I already fucking did, which is why—as Jack and I set out to travel those 2,807 miles all across this grand land of ours, I flat-out refused to listen to the hundreds of hours it was going to take for him to play the boxed set of some new Life of Benjamin Franklin, the first disk of which he'd unilaterally popped into the CD player, imagining in his mind's eye this epic scenario: A man, his bride, their handsome dog, all crossing the broad plains of a truly magestic country all the while being edified by learning more and more interesting things about one of our most interesting Founding Fathers about whom his bride simply didn't happen to currently give a shit.

So at about Mile One Twelve, with only 2,500 or so to go, I climbed into the back to ride with my dog and got out my Bose Noise-Cancelling Headphones and plugged them into my iPod and dialed up White Noise, going from Waves or Train Sounds going *clackety-clack* or sometimes listening to Krishna Das, singing Krishna, Krishna, Rama Rama, to drown out the Spoken Word spilling out the speaker for the next two thousand miles.

And for this I was not only pronounced "incurious," I was also told I swear too much.

I was pronounced "incurious" in a cornfield in Iowa where Jack and I had stopped to scream at one another while our dog was lifting his leg to pee on the Great All-American Corn Crop, also looking around to discover if some nicer people than we are might like to adopt him.

It was outside Iowa City, where Jack and I had the rest of the worst fight he and I have ever had over his turning left instead of right and I happen to know the cornfield fight took place outside Iowa City—though he disputes this fact—because it was in Iowa City that we officially stopped talking and did not speak another word to one another until we got to my aunt's house in Salt Lake City, Utah.

Things Proving Magic May Exist: That we lost our dog but survived, that we then found this one, not as pretty, maybe, but who has a better attitude, that a married couple such as we could move twice across this country lugging thirteen tons of books and live to tell the tale, though one has Control Issues and the other swears like a fucking trooper.

See, this, I figure, is how it goes: Some of us swear like a fucking trooper, whatever that is, while others of us do not. Some of us read the Potters, while others have no wish to, and all of this matters almost not at all.

All the digital is is a Yes, a No, all it really is is logic married to electricity and that is magic and it makes no difference that I say No to the Fucking Potters because a million zillion others have said Yes and so SJ reads them and so will Hazel and those who love these things will bring their enthusiasm and offer it as their gift to me.

I especially liked the latest one, I say to Sara Jane, lying.

Me too, she says.

I'm still looking down at her new doormat, still a little worried about the designator "127.0.0.1," which I'm thinking might be the name of a far-off star or galaxy.

Geek joke, SJ tells me and my dog. It's code, you know? 127.0.0.1 being a computer's own address, the one it uses when it talks to itself?

My dog glances up at me but I am looking away, I'm staring off and my face must hold that Miss Vandenburgh from Spain mix of perplexity and wonder because SJ feels the need to prompt me, and is opening her mouth to say it, though I shake my head just slightly and hold a finger up to say No need, as it's already lept by synapse between the two of us and my throat has tightened with that sweet sour twist like when you're squeezing lemons so we say nothing, yet we do then mouth the word together, this word being:

HOME

dog fight

After some months in the apartment in Emeryville with its long anonymous hallways, Jack and I moved to a little house on a hill overlooking the San Francisco Bay. Like so many Bay Area natives, I knew almost nothing about Point Richmond, which is so well tucked away it's known as the Hidden City—I'd never even stepped foot in the town until the day we came to look at our house.

The Point—as it is called by its natives—actually *is* out on a point that has isolated it in what is actually a geological cul-de-sac. Ours is the hilly landform jutting into the Bay that lies northeast from San Francisco.

Though it's now largely demarked by the wall made by Highway 580, The Point is where the city of Richmond began. Because the highway lies above the little town center, those streaking by on the freeway that carries traffic back and forth across the bridge into Marin County may not even notice the four blocks of the historic district, with its taverns and art gallerys, music festivals, and the hundred-year-old Hotel Mac that lie below.

About a year after we moved here, Jack and I went away on a car trip, leaving our son Noah to housesit and take care of Thiebaud.

We're loath to leave our dog in boarding, for obvious reasons, and Jack's so nervous about leaving him we do everything we can to take him, but we were at a writing conference where we couldn't have him.

It was early in August late on a Sunday evening when we got home, arriving just as night had closed in on the Point, where there are few streetlights. Folks are older here and tend to turn in early and the darkness on this moonless night was near complete.

We pulled up to the curb, the house was largely dark but the porch light was on. We got out and let ourselves in the back way. As soon as we'd opened the glass door into the mud room we could see Noah in the kitchen, kneeling beside Thiebaud, heavily panting, his leather lead still attached to his collar.

Thiebaud got in a fight, Noah said as he looked up. This just happened no more than five minutes ago.

A fight? I said. Thiebaud?

This was simply bewildering news, because this dog, unlike Whistler, was so eager to please. He also seemed to love everyone and everything, all people and every other dog he'd ever met, or so it seemed to me.

A dog fight? I said again. This dog? I simply couldn't imagine it: a dog fight involving an animal so laid-back he rarely got it up to bark?

It wasn't like we were only now discovering the quirks of our dog's personality, as he was now nearly nearly five years old, fully grown, weighing eighty-five pounds. Nor were we making those same mistakes we'd made with Whistler by allowing him to lose his dog-friendly skills in enforced solitary confinement with someone alone and working at home. We'd established the practice of taking Tee to day care at Metro Dog and to the dog park at Point Isabel to keep him socialized to other dogs.

Which dog? Jack asked.

That greyhound down the hill, Noah said, as he kept feeling all over our dog's head and body to check him out.

Some greyhound attacked him? I asked, as I too knelt.

Not really, Mom, Noah said. More mutual. More on this one, as he's the one who charged.

Some greyhound got into a fight with Thiebaud? I asked again, all this seeming so entirely unlikely I was having trouble processing the language.

Jack and I now were both kneeling beside our dog to pat and comfort him. Tee was excited to see us, wagging and making his little mewling sounds of ecstacy, and seemed entirely unharmed. This dog in a fight, I kept thinking, this dog, who can be so desparate and clownish in his need to please it's sometimes embarrassing? He will rush people climbing the Knob, throwing himself at them like they're his long-lost friends, will romp up to any pack he finds out there on the trails accompanied by the professional dogwalkers and join right in. Thiebaud's what we called a *sosh* in high school, honor students, perpetually running for office, good at sports, at dating, all but sickening in their need to be popular.

The people with the silverish Lexus SUV parked in their drive? Noah was telling Jack.

The pinkish Mediterranean? Jack asked, adding, John and Gene told me those people had it on the market for 1.6 but they took it off when it didn't sell. John and Gene are the town barbers, Jack gets his town lore from the barbers the way I depend on my next-door neighbor Anita Christiansen.

You know him, Jack said to me. Panama hat? the in-line skates?

That guy? I ask. The one in the ascot? Noah, that guy has something seriously wrong with him, I mean who has his greyhound pull him through the car tunnel on Rollerblades?

I was feeling the real need to comfort my son, as Thiebaud seemed fine, while Noah was in real distress.

How did this happen? Jack asked, and Noah began telling us how he'd taken our dog out on the trail from Keller's Beach along the shoreline where old railroad tracks lead to Ferry Point. They sat to watch the sun go down behind Mount Tam and were on their way back up to the house climbing the trail through the eucalyptus at the foot of Bishop, which dead-ends above the automobile tunnel at the bottom of our hill.

Thiebaud was on lead, Noah walking him at heel and under voice command, with Tee dragging his leash along. We were all taught to drop the lead by our trainer in the East as it's our holding on to it that often causes leash aggression.

Noah and Tee came upon the greyhound as they rounded the bend at the foot of our hill, standing alone in the middle of the dark street, a dog so tall and thin and pale, Noah said, that he at first took it for a deer. Before he could get Tee's leash in hand, our dog had already charged.

Thiebaud rushed up, the two dogs snarled, then went up on hind legs to tangle in the usual noisy way that sounds terrible and almost always isn't, especially when both dogs are hounds, as these two were. Hounds, our vet later told us, don't usually fight since they're so busy occupying the couch.

Over as quickly as it started, but not before the greyhound's owner emerged from the garage waving a stick over his head. He'd been in there doing something.

Shooting at a target with a bow and arrow, Jack said.

Noah had already got to the dogs, had Thiebaud's lead in hand. Though the dogs were no longer fighting the man with the stick came at them swinging it and yelling.

He carries it everywhere, Jack said. Some kind of carved African chieftain's staff. Uses it to ward off dogs who come near the greyhound.

An African chieftain's walking staff? I ask. Who *is* this cartoon person? I wonder.

When he came at me shouting I thought what he was swinging was a weed whacker, Noah said. He came at Thiebaud to hit him, but I got between them. Then he started waving it overhead like he was going to hit me and I didn't want to get into it with some old guy, so I brought Tee up short and walked on home, past all these people watching out their windows.

Noah was by now talking primarily to Jack, I saw. If life is war in the minds of men and boys—as it simply isn't in the hearts and souls of girls—it's my guess that there are myriad small tests of manhood going on all day long most of which women usually do not see. This exchange, between my husband and my grown son, was one of them.

I just realized that's the guy Anita's been telling me about, I said. She says he reads the stuff in our recycling can. She told me he once opened the front door to her house and Rollerbladed right inside.

My god, Mom, Noah said. I am so sorry I got Thiebaud mixed up with this asshole.

That's okay, honey, I said. Really, this isn't your fault, it isn't Thiebaud's either. Everything's going to be fine. This stuff happens, guy thinks he's living in a video game or whatever called Angry Greyhounds, anyway, he's so strange it stands to reason his dog's a little off too.

Dog's named Chomsky, Jack told us.

Chomsky? Noah asked. Who names their dog Chomsky? Then he looked down at Thiebaud, saying, Good dog, Tee! and Thiebaud wagged extravagantly at Noah's praise.

Our recycling-reading Rollerblading neighbor was named something Jack had been told by the barbers but could now not remember. He wasn't retired, rather he'd never worked, so he might be what

The Point had few of, which is legitimately rich people, our town not being stylish enough to attract more normal trust fund bohemians.

But this was neither someone dangerous nor particularly powerful as we were telling Noah, just another of the town's more than several eccentrics. Point Richmond—like any town at the end of the figurative road—will have its share of them.

And dogs just do fight, as we kept saying to him, but Noah still seemed almost obsessively worried. Noah is my own true son in that he assumes cosmic responsibility when things go wrong.

Nothing about this is your or Thiebaud's fault, I said again. Really, Node, dogs are just dogs, you know? They're simply animals.

You just don't like that one, do you, Thiebaud? Jack said to our dog. Those two have some private history, Jack said looking up at us. Tee just really does not like him and will stand on the rise next to the optometrist's and stare down the hill on a foggy morning, like he's watching for Chomsky to emerge. The greyhound wanders around in the eucalyptus grove like a ghost. When Tee sees him—or even senses that he's around—he'll strain and whine and stare meaningfully back at me, like he needs to get down there to take care of him.

Really? I ask. I have simply never witnessed *any of this* at all. Isn't it strange that the only dog Thiebaud has ever not liked is kind of a distant relative?

I think it's the spooky, skinny look that scares him, Jack said. He's wraith-like, maybe he looks half dead to Tee, or not enough like an actual dog?

Or maybe, Noah said, it's that someone named him something as fucked-up as Chomsky.

❧   ❧   ❧

The three of us talked as we were going in and out of the house, unloading the bags from our trip. We were then all inside standing in the foyer, as Noah stuffed his folded laundry into a duffle, getting ready to take off. Suddenly, the front buzzer sounded its horrible loud rasping squack. No one but UPS ever uses that buzzer—this was ten forty-five now on a Sunday evening and as the three of us stood staring at the door, it probably occurred to each of us to simply refuse to answer it.

But it buzzed again and Jack opened the door to a man in uniform: a Contra Costa County Animal Control officer now saying that our neighbor down the hill had called to report our dog, saying he'd been off lead and had rushed onto the neighbor's property to attack his dog.

What? the three of us said in unison.

Your neighbor, Mr. Bixbee, says your dog attacked his dog in his garage, the officer repeated.

That's just crazy, I said. That man's not trustworthy, I mean *look at him*. Who stands beside your trash reading manuscripts out of your recycling bin?

Jane, Jack was saying, his tone rising as it began to contain his Mr. Dickerson–type warning.

What he said is catagorically untrue, Noah said. I had the dog on lead, my dog was heeling beside me, he was under voice command and was never out of my sight, never anywhere near that man's property. The dogs met in the street as we came around the curve at least twenty yards from that man's garage.

Both dogs were off lead, Jack said. They met in the dark. They have some history, they simply spooked one another.

And the dog's owner Noah said was not out there with his animal to see what happened anyway, as his dog was roaming free. He only came out into the street when he heard the sound of the two dogs fighting.

The officer was back at his pad, now reading it aloud: Mr. Hudson Bixbee, the complainant, states that he was witness to the entire incident.

Again, Noah said, not true.

According to our son, this is not the way this happened, Jack said, in his most calm and forceful lawyer voice, and we believe our son.

That's right, I was thinking, you choose, Mr. Officer, take the word of our good boy or that of some douche who goes around on Rollerblades.

The officer knelt to look Thiebaud over, wrote down the numbers on his tags. I'll need to run your dog's tags, the officer said, as he stood, to make sure he has no other write-ups.

Write-ups? I asked.

Other incidents of aggression.

Of course there aren't any other incidents, I said indignantly, unless they write dogs up for acting ridiculous. This dog isn't aggressive. I mean, just *look at him!*

Thiebaud was panting, smiling, happy, as always, to be the center of attention. He also seemed to be watching the animal control officer, as if calculating how he was going to manage to get this guy to like him. You will be liking me, Thiebaud seems to think, if not now, then in a little while. The only person this has yet to work on is our son Sean.

The man took down our dog's tag numbers, checked his vaccination records, which Jack produced instantly, one clear advantage of living with a person so well-organized. Jack is so organized he's not only still in possession of the original Social Security card issued him when he was fourteen years old and got his first job bagging groceries at Scolari's Market in Orcutt, California, he can also not only immediately lay hands on it, he still has the original envelope it came in.

Then the officer went back out to his truck to talk on his radio, then abruptly—as we watched through the open front door—started his truck, turned it around in a three-point turn, and took off back down the hill in the direction of the Bixbees'.

He isn't very nice, is he? I said to Thiebaud. I think you'd be required to be much nicer to get to work with animals.

We all thought the man had gone back downhill to confront Mr. Hudson Bixbee, to challenge him for lying, but then the officer was back at our door a few moments later, saying our neighbor was insistent that our dog had been unleashed and running wild, that he'd charged up onto his property and attacked the greyhound in his garage.

It's an eight-year-old greyhound, the officer said. I saw the wound—it's a two-inch gash on his haunch.

The wound? we said.

Which that dog no doubt got, I said, when his owner starting whacking both animals with his medieval cudgel or whatever, but as I spoke Jack had already raised his calm Buddhistic voice so he was speaking over mine, saying WE WILL BE VERY HAPPY TO APOLOGIZE TO HIM AND TO ASSURE THEM THAT THIS WILL NEVER HAPPEN AGAIN.

They're upset, the officer offered.

As we too would surely be, Jack said.

They are very upset, the officer said, and I'd recommend that you not go down there. Their dog is going to need medical attention.

The man now stood looking down as he was writing out what seemed to be a traffic ticket.

Can you ask them to call us? Jack said, as he took the paper now being offered him, so we can figure out the vet bill between us in some fair way?

What? I was starting to say, *in some fair way?* That's not fair, there's nothing fair about any of this: Not only was my dog being villified but my son's truthfulness was being challenged by the word of some crazed club-wielding old guy who zooms around on Rollerskates shaking an African rain stick.

The officer was now talking, man to man, and only to Jack,

explaining that he'd made the determination that Thiebaud was in the wrong, that our dog—without question and by our own admission—had been being walked off lead in a public area and that he had, with his aggression, caused injury to another animal.

I honestly felt—at this point—aphasic, as if I could not get my understanding of language to catch up to the words being spoken. Thiebaud? This was somehow a joke, wasn't it? I was waiting, I believe, for someone to come up with the punch line.

But Jack was speaking in the cool, even negotiator's voice of Mr. Dickerson and Mr. Dickerson was telling the officer we would absolutely work cooperatively with the Bixbees to get their dog's vet bills paid, that we were so very sorry for all their inconvenience and heartache and now Mr. Dickerson was finally, finally showing the officer the door and he was finally, finally leaving, after saying one more time Animal Control of Contra Costa County hoped never again to even hear the name of Wayne Thiebaud Shoemaker ever spoken again.

It was only then, as I heard how ominous our dog's full name actually sounded, that it did finally dawn on me what Jack and Noah already knew: that this was, in fact, a very serious situation.

⚜ ⚜ ⚜

But in some of us the smart-ass is so deeply engrained in the DNA we simply cannot restrain ourselves and I am one of them, and my big brother Hank is another and my niece Lilah is another so maybe it has something to do with all of us having the surname Vandenburgh? So it was simply unfortunate for all that the next day, when eccentric Mr. Bixbee's equally eccentric vet called the landline at our house, Mr. Dickerson was at work and so was not home to answer it.

The vet introduced himself, saying he wanted to discuss Chomsky's treatment and to itemize the charges, then he started right in to enumerate these procedures, telling me the cost of each, rounding up, of course, all this totalling more than seven hundred dollars.

Seven hundred dollars? the smart-ass said. In American money? which was an ill-considered thing for her to say in that, from his name and by the sound of his accent, the vet was East Indian.

Allow me to begin again, the vet said, grandiloquently. Animal Control of Contra Costa County has adjudicated this and has found your dog to be entirely responsible for a wounding to my patient that is both grave and severe. The Hudson Bixbees have presented paperwork attesting to this, finding you wholly liable.

No they didn't, I said, and no he wasn't and no we aren't.

Excuse me? the vet said.

Sure, I said, I guess we might pay something. I mean I guess we'd maybe pay something or maybe might have, whatev, if it was like some reasonable amount, but seven hundred dollars?

I assure you, Mrs. Shoemaker ...

Not my name, I interrupted him to say.

Sorry, my error. Please forgive me. May I then speak with Mrs. Shoemaker, the vet asked, in the tone that means, May I speak to your mother?

Sure, the smart-ass answered. I'll give you her number, but I should also probably mention that Vic lives in Oakland with Richard, her subsequent husband, and believe me they won't be paying this stupid bill either.

Is there someone else I might speak with? he asked.

You could give Mr. Dickerson a try, I said, but he's not here.

Mr. Dickerson? the vet asked, by now completely confused.

Our lawyer, I explained, except he's not a lawyer.

The vet's silence had grown ominous.

Joke, I said. My husband is not, in fact, a lawyer, ha ha, nor is he named Mr. Dickerson. He doesn't even drive a lawyer car anymore, what with gas prices being what they are and ... ?

The vet's silence was now compounding.

But please allow me to give you the number of my husband, Mr. Jack W. Shoemaker, at his place of customary employment, where he is currently extremely busy in his extremely important job and maybe his person can pencil you in on his calendar.

And now you could palpably feel the vet on the other end of the line drawing himself up to full height to say:

I find nothing at all amusing in this exchange, Miss . . . ?

Vandenburgh, I said. Here, let me spell it for you. It's *B-U-R-G-H* and the *H* is actually important, as it shows it's Dutch, you know? though people may think I come from Spain.

The vet, who'd gone completely silent, breathed in audibly, breathed out, then began again.

Miss Vandenburgh, he said. I was informed by the authorities that you, as the aggressor's owners, would be paying for the treatment of what are actually very serious wounds to the Bixbees' dog, wounds that have required surgery, for which a general anesthetic was required, and both internal and external sutures taken. And it must be added that he is actually quite old and frail so it was impossible to safely treat him without first administering a set of extensive tests . . .

TESTS! I exclaimed. Of course there would be an extensive battery of tests to be done when two dogs meet in a dark alley and have a little dustup!

He breathed in, breathed out, and continued on, as if by script: But Chomsky has survived this surgery and now has a wound drain in place, there are also gauze bandages to be changed twice daily and the antibiotic shots. The aftercare also includes . . .

Oh I totally get it, the smart-ass agreed. Tests, wounds, sutures, all of which you must carefully itemize when you speak to Mr. Dickerson, whose number is . . . ? Are you ready with your paper and your crayon?

And the smart-ass is thinking up the quips she'll use as she's telling this story to her friends, how this blithering asshole of a vet called and was so clearly in cahoots with the owners of Chomsky Bixbee and how this whole trumped-up thing was just *so obviously* a case of Munchausen by Greyhound.

hidden city

We paid *the entire* vet bill, all of it, then heard little of Chomsky and his owners in the weeks that followed. Time rollicked onward, weeks rolling into months folding relentlessly into Dog Years, as they will when you're within a kinship system filled with animals and children.

And I now felt at first the same burn of shame that had haunted my own childhood, as The Vandenburghs came to be regarded as so obviously strange in our neighborhood, in those oh-so-conformist times. I now felt judged by our dog-owning neighbors, most of whom I did not know, imagining they were looking at my big black dog mistrustfully. No one actually ever said a mean word to me about him.

I published a book, wrote another, published that book too. Jack worked away at the job he loves and has always loved, doing the only thing he has ever done, which is publishing books that go in the Paradise Library.

We'd occasionally glimpse the Hudson Bixbees on our road, they now often drove their Prius, their tall dog curiously balanced in the backseat, the tiniest of the automobiles they owned, choosing this one, I was guessing, over the bigger ones in their fleet as a demonstration of their ecological advancement.

I didn't know the wife well enough to distinguish her from the other more-or-less-my-age blondes in this town, but I did see Hudson Bixbee alone. You couldn't miss him in the shining goldish white of his brimmed Panama, always a head taller than anyone else in this hat and elevated by his in-line skates. He'd always been conspicuous but I was now almost phobically aware of him. He did seem to turn up suddenly everywhere, at every community event, music festival, whatever gallery opening or church function or gala, any auction benefitting Washington School.

Nothing had changed and yet everything had: His family system and ours each now coalesced as a defensive pack, always keenly poised and aware of the other. Thiebaud was primed especially and was now hypervigilent, scanning the trails for any disturbance that might be a sign of them, sensing when the other animal, who lived only two blocks down the hill from us, was near. Now when we passed Hudson Bixbee and Chomsky in town as we drove through, Tee would just go crazy, barking and snarling wildly. This was both scary and shocking, as it was nothing Jack and I had ever before seen in him.

When we described all this to Dr. Otten, our vet said this was natural, that given any ten dogs you'll get two that will not get along for reasons that are often mysterious. But now that our dog had Chomsky in his scopes, he said, Tee was not likely to forget. Of course, he'd never forget, I said, Thiebaud has always remembered everyone and everything who's ever been important: Alice Vetter, though she might go several years between visits. He knew exactly where Dr. Otten himself kept his dog treats.

At the word *treats* my dog lifted his head and pointed as if to remind Dr. Otten, right up there! on that top shelf.

⚇ ⚇ ⚇

Point Richmond is a small community of five thousand or so in which people walk and hike the trails and bike and jog uphill from the village to the trailhead at the top of our road. These paths and tracks connect to a system of trails that will, one day, all be interlinked as the one continuous Bay Trail so you'll be able to circumambulate the entire San Francisco Bay.

Our town's center is its historic district, with its dozens of registered hundred-year-old buildings. We also have two good grocery stores, though Anita swears we haven't had really good meat in the village since Mr. Yamaguchi, the butcher, was shot by an armed robber in 1964.

We also have DeWitt's frame shop and gallery and a legitimate theater that puts on the kinds of crowd-pleasing musicals Jack and I never seem to get to, as well as two churches and the Tibetan Buddhist *sangha* that meets in what was once the stately Episcopal church, also Anita's Christian Science Reading Room. Point Richmond is home to a Starbucks, four or five good restaurants, including Brazilian, German, Mexican, and Thai, also the fake-meat vegan one in the barnlike building that's so sad and scary and empty that no one goes there but is kept open by funding from some spiritual group or cult that seems to have a following of two.

And from the end of April through mid-October we have a farmers' market that closes off several blocks of our little downtown on Wednesday afternoons. It's organized around a small triangular park in town that holds the community center, a small branch library and fire station, as well as the ten-by-twelve-foot building, one of the first to be built in The Point, once used to sell the lumber and other building supplies stored here, now run as a museum by the Point Richmond Historical Association.

One of the stalls at the farmers' market belongs to the owners of one of our town's more successful businesses, Bark Stix, the dog treat bakery where everything's made from organic ingredients. Our dog eats only Bark Stix products because he is—like his clinically sensitive owner—a little bit delicately put together in that any dietary upset causes his skin to break out.

The bakery is run by Kate Gebhart and Mim Drake, who are civic minded and offer their industrial ovens to roast the many turkeys the Methodists serve at their Thanksgiving dinner, which is attended not only by the true legion of Richmond's poor and homeless but also by the elderly and the lonely and by middle-class parents bringing their middle-class children to show them that the practice of breaking bread with people of all kinds is what knits a community together.

Mim and Kate are foremost among the greyhound rescuers in Northern California, rescuers who are notoriously well-organized and protective of these animals, of which there are an astonishingly large and growing number.

We got to know Kate and Mim after Thiebaud's fight with Chomsky. Kate actually delivered a fifty-pound bag of kibble to my house herself one day, essentially seeking me out. She was extremely kind to me, understanding, no doubt, my discomfort, in that Thiebaud had twenty or thirty pounds on Chomsky so it didn't seem, in retrospect, to be much of a fair fight.

Kate said she wanted to explain a few things she guessed I might need to know about the culture of greyhounds, saying greyhound people are a tightknit bunch who might remind you of the parents' network around a special-needs kids' school.

But if they seem hovering and overprotective, Kate said, it's only because greyhounds, as a breed, are misunderstood and have been so often mistreated. Despite careful screening in placements, the true needs of these animals will frequently go unmet, people getting them as long-distance runners when greyhounds are sprinters, or to go with someone's stylish furniture or to accessorize an outfit, and it happens not infrequently that greyhound rescue must then go out and rescue these dogs once again.

Chomsky hadn't come in through Bay Area Greyhound Rescue but from an organization she guessed was affliated with dog racing in Mexico. The greyhound people had, however, gone over to see the Bixbees to offer support, having heard about Chomsky's wandering in the street and in the eucalyptus grove above the car tunnel at the end of Dornan Drive and been told by Mr. Bixbee to get THE FUCK off his property.

The issue of keeping these dogs on lead was vitally important, Kate said, in that it's their nature to dash after anything they see moving away from them. Greyhounds will just automatically take off, blindly racing after whatever they pursue, which is why they fly around the track after the mechanical rabbit at such blurring speeds. This urge—prey drive at its purest—is so much a part of a greyhound's nature that even the most assiduous of training will not extinquish it and this is why a greyhound can never be trusted not to bolt.

And they are a tad high-strung and need a quiet environment, so home visits by greyhound rescue before placement will look for signs of instability of a household, which—she said and this was only her surmise—might be what was going on in the house down the hill from us.

Hudson Bixbee was often pulled by Chomsky through the car tunnel from the beach into town or there by the the bounce house at the Fall Fest, letting the little kids pet his tall and strangely beautiful dog, there by the food stalls or there in the front of the crowd right up by the band during a music festival, there having his picture taken with Chomsky in front of a sign reading:

NO DOGS ALLOWED

The phrase *No Dogs Allowed* evidently not applying to the Tidy Trust Fund Type Person, whose greyhound is, evidently, not a dog at all but something issued by the props department.

⚬ ⚬ ⚬

Between the time of the dustup—and I would not dignify it in my own mind by calling it a dog fight—I'd begun to run the trails in the hills above our house with a trainer named Nancy Allen Burns, whose specialty is healthy aging.

Nancy takes her workout group into our hills—a terrain technically known as a steep bluff coastal terrace habitat—where we trudge uphill wearing ten-to-fifteen-pound weight vests, jogging along the many miles of paths and switchbacks of the Knox-Miller Regional Shoreline.

Labeled the Potrero Hills on topo maps, I've never heard a soul refer to them as anything but The Knob or The Hills. The Point is the landform you see on either side of the cleft where the Richmond–San Rafael Bridge is sited on Highway 580. Ours are old and well-rounded hills, what's left of the most ancient range of mountaintops around here that were shoved up before the melting of the last Ice Age and include Angel Island, Alcatraz, and Mount Tam.

The hills to the right of the freeway heading toward the bridge belong to Chevron and are studded with the refinery's huge and numerous storage tanks, painted buff these days to make them maybe slightly less conspicuous. The hills to left of the freeway and surrounding our town are part of the East Bay Regional Parks system, which means you're allowed to have your dog off lead as long as he's under voice command.

Those of us in Nancy's group meet two or three times a week, warming up by doing Indian races along the wet sand of Keller's Beach, then starting up along a variety of trails toward the False Turret or Nichol's Knob, elevation 383 and directly up from our house to the south. The Knob has its stand of eucalyptus and bull pine, two picnic tables and benches. From there we have unobstructed views in all directions.

Looking southwest past Alcatraz you see the entire north side of the city of San Francisco, also the span of the Bay Bridge, footed in Emeryville, where we lived when Jack and I first arrived home in California. Then, as you turn, you see the buildings of downtown Oakland, in facing eastward, there are Berkeley, Albany, and El Cerrito spread out along the East Bay hills.

At the base of the Knob, looking down over the Port of Richmond, you find the old Ford plant, recently renovated as the magnificent performance space now known as the Craneway Pavillion, famous for its walls of glass windows, four stories tall and longer than a football field, also the still-active Shipyard Three, last of the four Kaiser Permanente shipyards that built nearly eight hundred ships during World War II. Here imported cars are off-loaded, then put onto auto transport trains run by Burlington Northern and Santa Fe Railroad. BNSF still uses the original East Yards to assemble the long trains that will carry cars back across the country. The railway tunnel lies parallel to the one cars use, the second bore through the base of the Knob leading from the town center out to Ferry Point.

Those who work out with Nancy are mostly women, all in our fifties, sixties, seventies. We are in such good physical shape from our hill-climbing and running—exercise for which you must qualify, as it is classed "strenuous"—that we must set our heart rate monitors way lower than our biological ages to keep these devices from issuing hysterical warnings as we jog up the switchbacks. We train in these hills in the mornings during the winter, then switch to evenings as the days grow longer.

And as I've done these workouts, I've gained not only in strength but in what I've lacked since the day my father died and I seemed to lose my place in society. What I've gained is more than fitness, it's a new sense of spiritual self-confidence; that I am not merely my own idea, that I live somewhere else rather than simply behind my eyes, that I am a physical being who belongs in the physical world. This means I need no longer hide inside my house, that I am welcome to come out of doors, that I too am invited to participate.

Nancy's class is called Outdoor Exercise. In the months, now years, since I joined, I've watched these hills, their foliage and wildlife, evolve with the subtle shifts that are California's seasons. Seasons as large-scale events are so much easier to see when you travel to other places. You need to witness a place habitually and over time before you begin to notice the differences one week to the next. I never much bothered to learn the names of plants in my native habitat: perennial bunchgrass, vetch, rattlesnake grass, red clover, mustard, French broom, live oaks, toyon, coyote bush, mesquite, all being what looked to me like what I'd have once called weeds.

And from my running friends—some of whom grew up in The Point—I've learned the lore, how the False Turret, against whose incline we do pushups, is the smoothly, regularly mounded small earthen shape put there by Kaiser to resemble an antiaircraft gun, exactly positioned at the mouth of the harbor to stand in defense of it.

The False Turret is reached either by switchback from the town-side or by climbing the Far Steps at Seacliff from Brickyard Cove. The hills there look out over what was orginally known as the East Bench, a tidal marsh traversed at high tide by scows loaded at Stockton and moving downriver through narrow shipping lanes laden with produce from the Central Valley, crossing the San Pablo Bay between the small twin rock islands called The Brothers to the east and The Sisters to the west.

Above us, a solitary hawk rides sideways on an updraft, a red-tail watching for rodents or smaller birds, ignorant of all our petty human concerns.

❧ ❧ ❧

Climbing a mountain is like writing a book—all it takes is the mind trick by which you hypnotize yourself into a state that's only suspension of negative belief. You don't need to yet believe you can write this book or climb that mountain, as these are frankly the accomplishments of other better people than you and I will ever be, those healthier in body and spirit, people who actually *know* something about something, who had good parents and were well brought up and so are not riddled by our lack of self-confidence. Better people than you and I are those who do these things, as they've got good concentration, better self-control.

Which is just so not true! All it takes to climb a mountain or write a book is the trick of mind whereby you allow yourself to be wrong for only as long as it takes to stop being entirely convinced you cannot do whatever is the secret thing you really very much want to do.

It's that tiny opening, the little gambit, whereby you allow your life to open to that thin little sliver of light that says, *There is possibility.* The first piece of this is simply admitting you have a dream, that this dream might still turn out the way you hoped it would, and it's the dream that lets you try to climb the hill or write the story, and it matters not at all that the entire time you're doing it you're saying, I can't, I wasn't meant to, with every breath pause and comma, with every footfall. *Of course you can't,* none of us can do any of these things, as they're way too hard for us! and we're too tiny, puny, babyish, too old, too fat, too frail, and—in my case—way too cursed by my lousy parents.

This is how it is always done by all of us, our secretly going *I can't,* all the while you climb the mountain, footfall by footfall, or write a book, sentence by crappy sentence, page after terrible page, day after discouraging day, week after futile week, living the life in which you and I are born to fail and fail and fail.

When we first moved to Point Richmond I *very literally* could not climb the 383 feet from Keller's Beach to the top of Nichol's Knob. I could not physcially accomplish this, so even the thought of taking this on as a challenge completely exhausted me.

The physiological reasons were several, all elaborately entertwined into a network of foolproof conviction: I'd been seriously injured when I was struck by a car in a crosswalk and had lingering physical issues and anyway I was now way too old to retrain myself out of my defeatist state of mind that came, essentially, from having had to endure such terrible parenting and all that terrible tragic stuff that happened to everyone I loved oh so long ago.

Climbing the Knob was, for a person like me, just too metaphysically challenging. I've simply never been that kind of active person. This is a direct inheritance from my mother, whose notion of heaven would be sitting comfortably on the banquet in some dark bar in Manhattan where you get together with all your glamourous witty friends to talk and drink and smoke cigarettes and speak of the books you were going to write and what was wrong with the books other people had already written and published while you and your friends were talking.

It was my mother who infected me with exactly that *New Yorker*-ish image of sophistication—all the Shiny Happy People doing all those obnoxiously healthy *outside* things in the Great Outdoors, So Forth, of the Wild West, where everyone was too provincial and illiterate to understanding the profound hopelessness that lies at the heart of everything that would render the punch line: *some coffee break.*

So it's still a shock to find myself in the wordless state of willingness that allows me to even mindlessly arise, sometimes in the dark, to find myself tying on my trail shoes so I can go out to climb a mountain, even if my own personal and most convenient peak is a hill rising to only 383 feet above sea level.

I've come to this realization so late in life: that it's hard to get up, hard to go out, hard to ascend, but for whatever reason I really want to do this, maybe because it evokes in me the mindless state of happiness I am almost entirely sure my mother never knew existed.

Why do we climb or write? Who really knows, but inch by inch, as the poet says, the snail climbs Mount Fuji.

ℵ ℵ ℵ

So one foggy Sunday, I take my dog—as I have literally hundreds times before—and we start out, heading up our road the long block and a half to the trailhead on our customary way to The Knob. The way has become habitual: I pull on my workout gloves, snap my water bottle into its carrier on my belt, check to see I have my watch that reads out BPMs transmitted by the Polar heart rate monitor I have banded around my chest.

I wear all this not because it's vitally necessary but because putting all this equipment together feels like a uniform. I'm not going for some leisurely stroll, but am off to do a kind of battle against my own determined will, as mine is a lifelong habit of indolence, depression, inertia.

I have my phone in its carrier on my belt, the kerchief I'll need to wipe my sweat, and always the fold-up water dish for Thiebaud that snaps into itself like an envelope.

My dog, on lead, walks along at heel, as he was professionally trained to in the East. We walk past the handmade house of Leslie the Optometrist up through the meadow where the Suicide Tree stands at the overlook. This is where a man from our town, an alcoholic according to John and Gene, tossed out of the house by his wife, hung himself in the first few months we lived here. The Suicide Tree once spooked me as it does no more.

This has been a walk and it now becomes a climb exactly there, in turning left at bull pine and ascending the trail. The trail there runs past the Ship House at One Crest Avenue built by the Ace Hardware guy on the narrow but very scenic lot at the top of our road, where a little cabin stood, so old it was historically protected but one night—again according to the barbers—was just mysteriously torched.

The Ship House is a pale gray blue and white clapboard—three stories tall, one room wide—and looks like it might sail away on the wind. Crest Avenue stops there at the park gate locked to all but official vehicles. The park road is called Marine View Avenue on maps, another of those official designations of a place that doesn't communally exist.

It's here at that gate a dog is legal off lead, so here I drop Tee's leash and turn him loose. And he does know—I have no idea what clues I give—whether we're headed up the steepest trail or will wind along around the longer but more gradual incline of the park service road. Today, he charges straight uphill, dragging his lead, stopping to pee and sniff for voles.

When he and I first began to make this climb, I'd need to stop at least twice to get another wind, also to gather the will to go on. Thiebaud would race away from me, but then lope back around, ever circling as if to say, We're alive out here! We can do it! Come on! Come on! Don't quit now!

I now hike straight up those three hundred or so paces, which takes only a couple of minutes, climbing to the top of the Knob. The climb is and will remain, in Nancy's parlance, effortful, which is what we strive for in our training, to do the thing that is just slightly too hard for us, to stay within our bodies, trusting our bodies to know that yes, we can, that *Si, se puede*, we can do this, that we are, in fact, doing it.

As we near the eucalyptus at the top we see a small cluster of people, the two couples who've hiked up along the more gradual south slope of the Crest Trail and are now on the Knob's overlook, able to see down into town but not quite able to visualize the best way to get there.

As we approach, I call Thiebaud to come, as he's trained to do, then reach down and take his lead. I do this always when we see folks ahead of us on the trail—I've seen the reaction in the faces of people who don't want a big black dog to come rushing at them in his crazily enthusiastic way, loping up to you in all his desperation for you to like him!

The folks at the top ask if the trail I've just climbed will take them back down toward town and I point the way down, showing them the road that starts at the Ship House, then winds off to the left beyond our sight, as this is where they'll hit South Washington. It's then three blocks downhill to town.

It's three in the afternoon on one of those grayed-out Sundays in late January, the fog, at midafternoon, is only now burning off. It's the Martin Luther King holiday weekend and Jack—who is not yet convinced he can or will ever join Tee and me on these trails—has gone off to his gym and to run errands in Berkeley.

At the top I sit on a bench facing west in the direction of Mount Tam, which I can't yet see through the fog. I'm hearing the clamoring of shorebirds and waterfowl who mate in the lagoon at Knox-Miller, but the birds too are still hidden by the fog.

I unfold Tee's canvas dish that clips to my belt, give him a drink, then take a long drink myself. He's lying next to me panting, my foot standing on his thin leather leash.

And now the fog is thinning, sunlight filtering in, the day becoming quickly dazzling: the luster of the water of the bay, landforms developing as I watch as they might in a Polaroid: Angel Island, Golden Gate Bridge, Raccoon Strait, the Headlands. I get my phone out of its holder to take a picture so I can text it to Jack—it is my most ardent wish that this man I so love will one day do this thing I love with me—and it is exactly as I'm taking this picture for him that Thiebaud senses what neither of us can see, makes a single throaty sound so low it's almost inaudible, and bolts. His leash slides from beneath my foot, him flying off with such force I'm yanked and have almost toppled, and with that my dog is gone.

He's flashed off to my right, nowhere near a trail, and there I see the upper torso of the small blonde woman I now recognize as the wife of Hudson Bixbee maybe thirty feet away, coming into view as she makes her way off-trail up the steep incline. She's bushwacking, walking straight uphill from the direction of town, her dog still below my line of vision.

I take off running, but the time slows, like when your soapy baby who's been sitting happily in the tub topples over and your grip slips, so he's underwater for no longer than a second but you do not experience time like this. Instead you're in the mind of your startled child, open-eyed, open-mouthed, for whom these few seconds underwater stretch outward toward eternity.

I've never before been this close to a dog fight, let alone in the midst of one, and it's as noisy as it is terrifying. I can't get there fast enough, but I am on top of them immediately and have waded into a giant commotion where the two dogs have arisen to bark and snarl viciously, then—and this feels like it's only a couple seconds later— abruptly quit. Now, they appear as they were, that's that, simply finished with one another, each standing only a couple of feet apart as if nothing's happened. I've grabbed up my dog's lead, am pulling his face toward mine, my hands on either side of his muzzle, blood suddenly all over him.

Right in the middle of all this is a woman screaming. She's screaming and she keeps screaming. She's screaming not at the dogs, who are no longer fighting. Instead she's screaming at me:

THIS IS ALL YOUR FAULT, she screams. I WANT TO

HURT YOU, she screams. THAT DOG OF YOURS SHOULD BE SHOT.

Blood is gushing from Thiebaud's muzzle, it's now all over my hands as I hold his face to look at him. There is also blood on the rump of her dog, blood wherever I touch, but my mind—I am calm and reasonable in emergency—tells me Tee's is only a mouth wound, that it will bleed like hell but is also superficial, so I say to her in a quiet voice:

I understand that you're upset, but you and I both need to calm down so we can help our animals.

CALM DOWN! she screams. HOW DARE YOU TELL ME TO CALM DOWN! YOUR DOG JUST ATTACKED MY DOG FOR THE SECOND TIME!

You need to stop screaming, I say. You're scaring them.

STOP SCREAMING! she screams. I WILL NOT STOP SCREAMING UNTIL THAT DOG OF YOURS IS DESTROYED.

And with that she clips the lead on Chomsky and runs on down the the hill.

I look at Thiebaud, who's been bitten in the face but for whom I am feeling not the slightest twinge of sympathy, and say aloud, Now what in the *fucking* hell was all that all about? Then: Do you have even the slightest idea of what you've just done?

Thiebaud's panting, his teeth are bloody. I wipe my eyes, stinging with sunscreen and blurred by the blood of animals and by my own sweat and by the tears that are flowing now with a mix of terror and anger. I can still hear her screaming as she runs down the hill but now there's another sound I only faintly recognize, the Polar heart rate monitor on my wrist bleeting danger! danger! danger!

As we head downhill I am frantically texting Jack on my phone: pls come home now! t & chomsky got into another fight—please come home!!!!! we need you!!!!

I send it, then text him again immediately. PLS COME HELP ME! I DONT KNOW WHAT TO DO!

Oh, no, I'm saying, but I'm not exactly talking to my dog. Oh, no, oh no, I'm moaning this aloud, mopping his face then my own face with the same bloody neckerchief, splashing us both with spurts from my water bottle, spurting it right into his bleeding mouth.

I am so frightened I'm sick to my stomach, but I'm also furious with my dog, also feeling all but betrayed by him. I feel like a woman must who's just learned the husband she thought devoted has been chronically unfaithful. I sleep with this animal, this animal is my intimate, but I do not—not in this moment—even vaguely understand who or what he has become.

I bring Thiebaud into the house via the glass door into the mud room, then sit him by the sink in the kitchen so I can look him over, wiping at his face with a dampened dish towel. The worst wound seems to be a half-inch nick at the corner of his mouth but the bleeding has already nearly stopped.

I call him into the bedroom and lay out bath towels over the bedspead and hop him up on the bed to stay while I'm gone, then close the door on him, without uttering a single word of comfort, go back out the same glass door. I am dressed exactly as I was, am still texting Jack as I go, now racing downhill, headed for the Bixbees' house on Bishop.

My fingerless trail gloves are bloody but I don't stop to take them off.

Their gate is open, the front door standing open too. Inside the tiled foyer, Hudson Bixbee is kneeling beside his dog, tending Chomsky by dabbing at his side with a wet washcloth.

I am so so sorry, I say, as I come up and stand in the doorway. The man glances up at me, says nothing. I step forward, entering tentatively. He's putting Neosporin on a bloodless wound that runs a couple of inches along Chomsky's flank. This wound looks shallow and so eerily matches the one described to me by the vet in the first incident I'm having a dreamlike sensation that hovers in the vicinity of déjà vu.

I stand near, looking down at the dog—I've never before been this close to Chomsky. The greyhound looks so sadly old, a dog so thin his bones show through, his skin not only nearly hairless but also transluscent, his fragile hide nicked and scarred and scraped all over the back and haunches, as if this is just the latest in what has been a series of incidents.

Eyes filling, sick at really seeing how frail and tragic this animal seems—why would my young and healthy dog develop such an intense hatred for such a helpless-seeming animal? How could Chomsky have ever registered as any kind of threat to Thiebaud, none of this even beginning to make sense.

I am so sorry, I tell Mr. Bixbee. I saw the whole thing, Chomsky did nothing to provoke Thiebaud this time. My dog just rushed him. I am so very sorry, I say again.

So you'll pay the vet bill? Bixbee asks, looking up at me almost shyly from under the bill of his hat. It's only now registering that maybe it's a little strange for his man to be wearing his hat inside his house.

Of course, I say, but if you could just please avoid calling animal control? If you call animal control, they'll impound my dog.

Trying to see, the man mutters, if we can possibly avoid that ... ?

I am offered only this tiny piece of hope but it seems to be enough to break my heart. I hear myself seem to breathe in, then breathe out in what sounds like a rattling sob.

We'll take him to his vets' in the morning, Hudson Bixbee tells me, and we'll see what he says. He then says something inaudible, then his voice simply trails off.

Thiebaud isn't a mean dog, I say. Honestly, it really is just something between them, something in the chemistry of these two animals.

And now I suddenly want to reach out to touch the greyhound in comfort, yet I don't. Instead I say his name: Oh, Chomsky, I say, I am so so sorry my dog hurt you.

Hudson Bixbee doesn't answer but he also doesn't argue. Instead he simply continues to dab at the bloodless wound that looks like a crease etched by a sharp fingernail and it's right here that I feel the gauzy curtain part as I'm being admitted to my own version of Wonderland.

This is as it always is, my fictional world simply irresistibly beckons and I am welcomed and enwrapped in hope and suddenly I'm rewriting history and thinking, What a *kind* man Hudson Bixbee is and how seriously I've misjudged him and then the door to the interior of the house bangs open and there she is again, this diminutive blonde person, who does not rev up to scream, instead, enters screaming:

I WANT TO HURT YOU! she screams. LIKE THAT DAMNED DOG OF YOURS HURT MY DOG. YOU NEED TO BE PUNISHED. WE WILL NOT STOP THIS TIME! WE WILL NOT STOP UNTIL THAT DOG OF YOURS IS PUT DOWN.

You know what? I am saying this in my calmest tone, the tone I developed growing up with a crazy mother. It actually *is* against the law to threaten people with violence.

GO AHEAD! she says, CALL THE POLICE! only inches away and screaming directly into my face, her miniature fists pumping the air like she can barely resist the urge to strike me. YOU'D JUST BETTER HOPE THEY GET HERE QUICK!

Liz? her husband asks, in a small and defeated voice, and she—without turning away from me—yells, SHUT UP HUDSON, then screams back at me: WE ARE GOING TO PURSUE THIS LEGALLY. THAT DOG OF YOURS IS A MENACE. I WANT HIM EUTHANIZED AND I WANT YOU TO GET THE HELL OUT OF MY HOUSE!

Oh my god, I'm thinking, as I back away from her and out of the front gate and start back up the hill, in this particular *folie à deux* down the hill from us, it's *that man* who is the rational one.

pda

Jack was just driving up as I got home, I fell in automatically and began to help him in going back and forth from the car to bring in groceries, moving nervously and from the powerful need to do something and there being nothing much to do.

He and I talked as we went in then came back out, Jack hearing the story in all its detail, then kneeling beside Thiebaud to check him out and all this taking on the sense of our having lived through this calamity before and our never getting better at it.

The name of the woman who had threatened me was Dr. Elizabeth Medina, psychologist rather than MD, as we'd recently been getting through the John-Gene-Anita rumor mill. She had in no way really frightened me; it was simply startling that she'd acted as she had. Who does that? I kept asking Jack. What kind of educated woman stands in front of another woman—her neighbor!—and threatens her with physical violence?

The Bixbee-Medinas were still almost entirely mysterious, maybe she had two grown children, maybe boys, perhaps from a previous marriage. Maybe she was the one, someone thought, who earned hundreds of thousands of dollars a year at San Quentin counseling Death Row inmates.

It was Sunday afternoon, the next day a holiday, we spent that evening pacing from room to room as we talked to each of our kids on the phone, this turning out to be in no way a particularly comforting activity.

Noah and Eva were each quiet as I told the story and as I spoke the Bad Dog Mom vibes came twisting around my ankles, thick as roping vines invasive as the kudzu overgrowing the swampy South so fast you swear you can hear it growing, and Sean is a hard ass who never did like dogs and hasn't loved a cat since Coltrane died and is now the father of not only Hazel, who needs things, but the twins Katrina and Marcel, and they do too, and so has decided all pets are a complete waste of time and money ever in short supply and he was anyway making dinner and had to go. And Demian, up in Seattle, was completely sympathetic because D is always sympathetic, but he's never had a dog, so didn't really get it, besides he's so conflict-averse as we told him this story he kept yawning and yawning not because he was bored but because D's so softhearted he just really could not bear the horror of what we were saying.

Jack and I were sleepless all that night, jumpy and apprehensive until the phone rang in the late morning, its being Chomsky's vet's front office person calling to say the dog had made it through surgery and was now in recovery. She was calling to ask for our credit card so she could get the billing started, saying this time it was likely to be more than a thousand dollars.

One thousand dollars? Jack asked, then—in his Mr. Dickerson voice—said he'd like to speak to the vet. Sitting with him at the dining room table, I looked down and shook my head, knowing speaking to the vet to be just such a terrible idea, as I'd have reminded Jack, had I had the chance. You don't want to speak to someone who had it in for you even before you accused him of writing with Crayolas.

When the vet came on the line, Jack got about as far as, Yes, this is Jack Shoemaker, then fell silent behind the onslaught. Yes, I know,

but ... yes, we do realize ... then Jack waited, occasionally drawing
question marks on the pad he'd set out, as if to question the validity
of this whole enterprise. Wound track??? he wrote, then ... touch
and go ...???? then went back to listening. Finally, as the vet was
finishing up, Jack wrote, Bite me.

No, not at all, Jack said at last, but I did want to ask why it's so
much more than last time, when my wife, who saw the injury, says
it looked like the dog was simply grazed on the haunch by one of
our dog's claws ... ?

And here the vet simply exploded! He was so loud I could hear
the clipped precision of his accented words distinctly, asking how
dare my husband question his judgement and professionalism?
Saying this was no mere nick or graze, but a gash, an open gaping wound, a violent wounding, then offering details of this wound
again, how it measured so and so many centimeters, requiring so
and so many sutures ...

Oh for fuck's sake, I said in the vague direction of the large black
dog lying on the floor asleep near us. I spoke without really looking at him, as I still was not talking to my dog, was even making it
my point to gaze off when he looked up at me now, as if to ask a
question.

Avoiding eye contact is a tactic I adopted when I was the mother
of teens and would catch myself thinking, I love you, of course, and
would die for you without question, but right this second I really
just do not like one single thing about you.

⚘ ⚘ ⚘

Why? I kept thinking, why? getting always nowhere, as I just
couldn't begin to understand the first thing about it. Meanwhile,
in this little town, word was spreading, how up on the Knob that
big black wild dog hurt poor ancient tottering Chomsky *once again*!

I believed I could actually hear this town—where I'd begun to make friends—turning against us. Jack would be immune to this, as he enjoys a certain measure of isolation and so might not even notice. It's really only women and children who have this desperate need of the society of others. I learned this as a kid as our parents each got worse and their more obvious bizarrities became more and more apparent. My mother was the more flagrant of the two, going out sloshed to the main street of town to drunkenly proclaim: PUBLIC OPINION NO LONGER WORRIES ME. This kind of behavior caused my brothers and me to be at first looked at funny, then talked about, then teased, and finally cast out of our first community, which was made up entirely of dogs and children.

Jack would be able to soldier on alone and I'd try to do so too, but I'm too much like my dog—a warmhearted convivial sosh—and so now we'd be required to move. We'd need to move again though we'd already moved way too many times, and are forever coming into some new town, and having to act all gregarious and interesting and nice, trying to trick people into liking us.

We'd need to move because public opinion does worry me and I knew I was not capable of living in a place where my dog—by his very nature so friendly and eager to please—was feared and hated.

It seemed to me that the dogwalkers who came along our block had begun to pick up their yapping Purse Dogs and clutch them to their breasts as they swished hurriedly by—or so I was imagining. I had to imagine all this as I was no longer leaving the house or even looking out our front windows.

Jack, true to form, was still walking Thiebaud, as he always had, oblivious to how he and Tee were being regarded. My husband is a man of calm habit. The two of them walk out together two or three times a day, heading up our road and along the path through the meadow, then up the asphalt park road to the overlook.

I had tried to go outside but could not make myself. Instead, I would put Tee into our fenced backyard, watch him squat or lift his leg, then I'd immediately bring him in again. I was so mad at him I didn't really want him near me but was also so afraid for him I couldn't stand his being out of my sight, so I pulled the blinds down at the back of the house to close it off from the glare of the bright bowl of aluminim now radiating off the Bay and huddled with him on our bed, then pulled a pillow over my head.

⁛ ⁛ ⁛

By Tuesday afternoon, Jack is back at work and we are $1,087.54 poorer and I am too distracted to get anything done. I put my dog, whose name I no longer say, into the yard for a moment, then have him hop on our bed and shut the door. It's still getting dark early but I will not turn on a light for him or hit the button on the radio so he can listen to NPR, as Jack always does, as these are gestures of comfort that I'm simply not going to afford my dog.

With the precision of my trauma-locater bull's-eye I know I will never again be able to go out to climb the Knob, but I am also too anxious to sit around. I get ready to go swim laps at Point Richmond's newly renovated town plunge but am so distracted I must pack and repack my swim bag over and over again. It's just as I go out the kitchen door, just as I'm pulling the door behind me—I realize I've forgotten a towel, so I go to the front porch to let myself back in and this is when I notice the buff-colored card lying on Jack's grandmother's white wicker table, next to the red geranium in its clay pot.

Please contact Contra Costa County Animal Control, the card reads, regarding. The box that's checked says: *PDA. Ongoing investigation of your Potentially Dangerous Animal.* In the line provided below the officer has written in by hand: *Your dog has attacked your neighbor's dog for the second time.*

I use my iPhone constantly and always have it on me. It works for me like a miniature laptop—I've written chapters of books on it, it's my soul, I read *Anna Karenina* on it in bathrooms, live by the light of its halo, but for whatever reason I truly hate the act of talking on it so please never, ever call me and if you do please don't be hurt that I will never answer it, okay?

I don't ever consider calling Jack. I don't call him because I'd have to go through the entire electronic jungle gym whereby I'd have to be waiting and then hitting numbers and/or pound symbols or maybe doing it wrong and hitting the asterisk, then dialing the extension I actually do not remember and who needs all this when he won't answer anyway because he's always in a meeting.

So I text him: Call me. I say nothing about why.

Riding massive waves of panic, I now go back inside the house and set this card next to his chair in the living room where he'll be sure to see it when he gets in, then take my bag and head down to the pool. I'm going ahead to swim not because I want to but because I'm now having to try really hard not to lose my mind. Swimming works better than other forms of exercize because it's completely private. Also, since you're lying face-down as you go back and forth in a lap lane, this is one place where no one can be completely sure it's you.

I swim laps as I used to do when my son and daughter were younger and only independent enough to have entered into that state of peril and risk over which I had no parental control. It was then I happened upon the most helpful advice ever offered by any-one: *Pray without ceasing.* Pray without ceasing is what Jesus said to his disciples in the garden at Gethsemane, those who loved him and knew they were just about to lose him.

This is the way I pray: I'll swim one length and—if I've not yet been drowned by my own anxiety—I'll do a flip turn, then swim another length. As I swim I feel the panic rising but I take the energy of fear and worry back and forth across the water and into the wall with me. I hit the wall doing a flip turn, feeling the terror throughout my body, but am working on the act of channeling this energy into something physical that can drive me forward instead of killing me.

I swim, turn, breathe, and all the while I'm keeping my face in the water and am going pleasegodpleasegodpleasegodpleasegod.

I am swimming, counting, turning, and as I do I'm becoming increasingly magical, trying to force the months between the two fights to be at least eighteen. Eighteen is a magic number I've just come up with. If I can get it to be eighteen months between incidents, I'm guessing we might stand a chance. Hell, it's been *months*, I see us saying to Animal Control of Contra Costa County. Aw, come on, man, dogs will be dogs, won't they? A dog gets to have a fight every year and a half or so in a free country, doesn't he?

But in fact eighteen months have not elapsed, so I'm also strategizing on how we will beg or maybe bribe one of our kids into taking him to live in a different town, but three of our four children are in Berkeley, which is in Alameda County, a different jurisdiction with maybe even worse rules regarding dog behavior, and anyway Sean and Eva have cats and Noah's not allowed, besides all three vaguely disapprove of Jack and me, probably because of our checkered pet history, acting like any animal we've ever had wasn't really safe with us.

The only one who doesn't vaguely disapprove is Demian, who lives in Seattle with his wife and little daughter and their cat Gracie. D would never consider having a dog himself, though he doesn't seem to mind if his dad and I do.

Or we could ship Tee back to Washington, DC, to live with Alice Vetter—Alice will of course take him, except Thiebaud just does not travel well. This dog, in fact, travels more poorly than I do, so I'll be the one who'll need to drive him there in the car. I'll set out for Washington first thing in the morning, driving him all those same 2,987.4 miles there myself and maybe end up living at Alice's again, as I obviously can't live here, but first I'll need to stop off at the Kaiser pharmacy to pick up a refill on my sleeping pills.

Swimming, counting, planning, bartering with God—if God

will please just spare my dog one more time, I will at least make a concerted effort to believe in Him—consumes the better part of an hour. I do all this while completely convinced none of it will work. I am completely certain this is what will now happen: Jack and I will have our dog taken away from us as we are forced by draconian law to stand passively by.

That we will now lose Thiebaud was preordained by The Three Fates long ago, back when the history of Jack and Jane and their terrible luck with pets was being written as pure and unadulterated tragedy. We've had such bad pet luck we've become famous for it among our friends, our bad pet luck nearly rivaling the bad luck we've had trying to cross the street together in a crosswalk where Jack and I've both been hit by a car not once but twice, prompting one of his wiseass friends to tell him, You don't cross in a crosswalk, Jack, that's where the cars go to look for you.

This bad luck of ours with pets has now taken on such alarming and cataclysmic proportions as to create its own almost mythic circumference, its own weather, the kind of luck that will begin to compound, begin to cause itself. Our bad pet luck is now threatening to become absolute, our having tragically lost not only Whistler, but both of the two cats Jack and I have had together, and all to cruel and sudden circumstance. It is all too sad to behold, too sad to speak about, too sad to bear, that this poor dog once saved us and we'll now be able to do nothing to save him.

None of this, not a single piece, has ever felt in any way fair to me, that Jack and I have never been allowed to accompany an animal—as other people seemed to—along on the regular journey of temporal migration that you conspire to make as a kinship system, knowing one of you might be lost but the others will be there to hold you up, to help to stagger bravely on.

Instead, our pets have all been snatched from us in youth and health when there was nothing wrong with them. The loss of Eva's cat Gris Gris was the first of these and it happened immediately upon our arrival in Washington—Gris Gris's simply vanishing out a window—and this cast a pall over our arrival, but there was simply nothing to compare the compounding and rhyming grief of losing first our dog Whistler, then her cat Phoebe within the same week, the unfathomable coincidence that helped propel us out of West Virginia to move those three thousand miles home.

It is Phoebe's death that was so awful as to become the incident about which he and I simply never speak.

⚩ ⚩ ⚩

Though we haven't arranged for Jack to pick me up, he's there parked in front as I leave the plunge. As soon as I'm seated in the car he tells me he's already talked to the Bixbee-Medinas and that they're being no more reasonable than before. Though Jack had technically been speaking with the husband on the phone, Hudson Bixbee had gone electively mute in that weird way he has, silenced as always by the screaming of his over-the-top wife in the background about how TRAUMATIZED! they all are and how they were pursuing LEGAL REMEDIES! in getting our dog destroyed, as they no longer feel safe in THEIR OWN NEIGHBORHOOD!

The dog fight was on Sunday afternoon, this is Tuesday evening, and Jack has already called to arrange a visit with the animal control officer in the morning. He says he'll stay home with Thiebaud and me and not go back to work until this matter is resolved. This is intended to comfort me, I know, but it doesn't. My husband normally does have an almost uncanny ability to get out in front of impending disaster, except in the case of our pets, as he and I have each proved equally as impotent in trying to save our poor doomed animals.

It's here, as we're parked in front of the plunge, that Jack turns to me and in the most heartbroken voice I've ever heard him use, says, Jane, I don't know if I ... and here his voice breaks and he must start again: I don't know how to make this turn out the way we ... ?

What he's unable to bring himself to promise is exactly what the two of us keep on not-so-secretly expecting, that is, for this life of ours together to provide each of us with a happy ending.

⚜ ⚜ ⚜

All this felt almost incomprehensible—as if the world had tilted and been emptied as it will in the dream of Time where it—and you—are frozen and you can't get yourself to move.

There really now seemed to be nothing to do, so Jack proposed that we go ahead and do what we'd planned, which was meeting our friend Annie Lamott for dinner in Larkspur Landing. We always meet her at this certain Japanese restaurant we all like because it's right over the bridge into Marin from us and almost exactly the same distance from Annie's house in Fairfax.

Jack always wants to go eat because he, under stress, suffers from whatever is the opposite of a loss of appetite, even as he, under stress, also starts to become almost belligerently methodical. A person needs to eat, he insists, we all might benefit from the comfort provided by sitting down to a regular meal.

Annie looks up from the table where she's already been seated, and immediately says, Okay, what's up?

I sit right next to her and, as she and I always do, we kiss hard on the lips. Her lips are always a little dry, also muscular, so they have this particular Annie-like resistance and texture that states how emphatically she means this.

Horrible, I lift my palms, held upward, to show how totally we are defeated.

Kids? she asks. She and I are mothers, the only way we get from one day to the next is to pray without ceasing.

We are going to maybe lose our dog, I say, immediately hearing how over-the-top this sounds. Still in saying it aloud, I realize I do believe it: Jack and I may lose our dog!

Thiebaud? Annie asks, turning to Jack, who nods, and he and I then begin taking turns in telling her the story, him terse and grim, me struggling to rein in my need to overemphasize how terrible this woman is, how violent her language, how bizarre the husband seems. Can it be that real live people would really act like this?

As we speak my panic's rising, sped along by the quick pulse of shame. I am ashamed of my dog, ashamed of myself for owning him, and now this shaming story is being told aloud and in such detail and even our most loyal and accepting and dog-loving friends will feel the need to pull away. Annie will no longer want to walk dogs with me, I know, Lily and Bodhi needing to keep their safe distance.

Because I saw it, I say to Annie, and Thiebaud was in the wrong, the greyhound did nothing to provoke him.

You don't know that, she says. Dogs are dogs. They have their own doggish reasons for what they do.

The sheer bad luck of it, Jack says, that it's those same people and the same dog twice. And they have this wing-nut vet who's so concerned he'll be busted for his flagrantly overcharging us that he felt the need to call animal control to reemphasize how life-threatening this ICU-ish scratch of Chomsky's is.

Horrible, unkind, vindictive, I say. He's completely odd—who carries a rain stick to clobber other dogs with? and she's a clinical psychologist . . .

Of course she is, Annie says, now bent over her phone and already texting.

. . . and she's completely heartless, I go on, which maybe comes from the work she does in wherever hellhole it is that she works in, Quentin maybe? maybe with Death Row inmates?

You know, *Joie*, Annie mentions as she looks up from her texting, I don't think it is the neighbors who get to decide these things. We had this truly vicious Pol Pot–ish dog on Chestnut who attacked everybody's animals and no one ever took a vote on how we felt about this dog's future. Because a dog's basically your property. He's your dog, he might be valuable.

Thiebaud isn't valuable, I say.

He's valuable to you.

He was, I say, before he turned mean and started to cost us thousands of dollars in vet bills.

Thiebaud stays your dog until some court or judge or official agency stipulates otherwise, Annie says definitively, then she adds. Dogs are dogs—they go by their own system of animal justice that we can only guess at. I know Thiebaud, so I suspect he has his reasons.

Annie's busily texting as she speaks and now begins telling us who the person is she's texting and how he or she is going to help us and Jack and I are both trying to smile gratefully but when we raise our eyes to one another's each sees the same grim mask of terror and hopelessness.

All this effort of Annie and her friends will do no good, as Jack and I both believe. This will not turn out okay, as it never has in the history of the two of us and our animals. We are simply pet cursed and can't seem to shake it.

And he and I have been through this all before, the authorities coming in the dead of night to take an animal of ours and there being nothing we could do stop them. They arrived with an order saying they got to take our cat, they caught Phoebe and crated her, drove off, and we never saw our cat again.

⚜ ⚜ ⚜

We are eating edamame and trying to distract ourselves by speaking of other things, our work, the kids, how Sam and Jax are doing, but we keep circling back to Thiebaud.

There are just so many way-worse dogs than Thiebaud, Annie

says. So many dogs have done such worse dog things and they got to live long and happy lives.

You think? I say, completely unconvinced.

That pit bull down the street from us on Chestnut who dug under the fence to get out time after time? Someone had to knock him over the head with a Weber to get him to stop killing their dog. That pit got another chance.

That's in Marin, I said. Animal Control is no doubt nicer in Marin. Besides Thiebaud has already had another chance.

Annie was trying to buck us up, even as she kept busy texting various people. She's lived in Marin County her entire life and keeps looking up from her texting to explain exactly how this or that important person is going to help us, all this sounding certain and highly informed and emphatic, except there's really nothing Annie can do because Jack and I will never be convinced.

She keeps telling us how everything will proceed, how things are going to happen, how So-and-So will be texting her back in just another minute, this person *more than happy* to help us. She's being in all ways encouraging so we nod and listen and pretend to believe her.

And the kids judge us, I tell Annie. They not-very-secretly believe that all our pet tragedy comes from our basic suckishness as animal parents.

Fuck that, Annie says, all Thiebaud was doing was acting like a dog. Dogs *get to* act like dogs, they *get to be dogs,* which means they're different from us, they also get to make mistakes.

Annie starts telling us a story we've never heard before about her dog Bodhi's getting into trouble. Bodhi's a rescue, had been abused, was therefore a little iffy in the aggression department and had accidentally bitten someone who may have been a human person. He actually may have accidentally bitten even *a couple* of human persons, she says, then adds: Bodhi may have even accidentally bitten me, through no fault of his own, and he was just so *entirely* sorry afterward, going, Oh, Annie, I am so so sorry! I got you mixed up with that douche who used to own me . . .

And he's also bitten another unnameable somebody, Annie adds, someone who is actually such a monumental pain-in-the-ass she deserves to be bitten by at least a spider or a mosquito every day or so, which isn't a very Christian thing to say but then Jesus forgives us for this kind of observation since people like that really do tend to try His Jesus-y patience.

We can know only this: Dogs know things we don't know, they also never forget. They also make mistakes. Bodhi made a mistake when he bit me, so he had to go back to Karin Grahn's to be retrained. And Thiebaud's messed up one too many times so he's going to go to Karin Grahn's too—I've been texting her, Annie says brightly. So far, no answer.

Annie, I know, I'm saying miserably. We can forgive him, of course, we've already forgiven him and all this would be halfway to being largely forgotten except it's turned official. Thiebaud's already had his official warning and now he's been officially reported for PDA for the second time in the same eighteen-month period which makes our dog not only a PDA but a serial offender . . .

No one ever said anything about an eighteen-month period, Jack says.

But it stands to reason, doesn't it? that there'd be some kind of probationary period after which a dog's record is expunged?

There isn't, Jack says definitively. He's a dog, not a minor. Tee's records will never be sealed and this is why we are going to have to move out of Contra Costa County.

Move to Fairfax, Annie says, texting.

All right, I say, though I have no wish to move to Fairfax except that maybe animal control is nicer in Marin and we will actually move anywhere to save the life of our dog.

But Annie, I say, hearing how my voice sounds just this side of hysterical—I just can't get my mind around the way he's acted. Tee has been socialized, he gets the highest marks at day care at Metro Dog, he romps with all kinds of dogs off lead at Point Isabel, if anything he's too friendly. He has never not liked a dog until Chomsky.

It's probably nothing more than Chomsky's wandering up and peeing on Thiebaud's lawn one too many times, she says.

As our food is served and we start eating our sushi and salmon teriyaki the answering texts start blurting in, each one lighting up the glass face of her phone. She reads some of these texts aloud to us and the best are the worst-case really Bad Dog Stories, where dogs have acted way more terrible than Tee, so much worse than Bodhi, yet they got to live. These are the worse-than-even-the-pit-stunned-by-barbecue stories, the standard poodle accidently locked by a groomer in the same room as the little terrier he killed in less than a minute, the Rott who put another dog's eye out, then attacked another dog, then yet another and did have to eventually have to be put down but only after he'd run through oh so many chances and his owners had finally exhausted all kinds of legal rigamaroles.

These texts come in also offering referrals and helpful suggestions, they are bounding in, streaming to us via Annie's contacts, all these people who want to help us because they are DOG PEOPLE and know exactly what it is to love a dog as we do. The stories all say the one same thing, as they arrive by bing and rattle against the tabletop, that Jack and I are not alone.

But the person who is really going to help us has not yet texted back because she doesn't text, as I'll later find out, and is often out of cell phone range in the wilds of Marin or Sonoma counties. This is the dog trainer Bodhi went to after his teeny mistake, the biting incident that may have actually been incidents, plural.

Karin Grahn is famous in the North Bay—Marin and Sonoma counties—for saving dogs way more hopeless than Bodhi, those in way worse trouble than Thiebaud, if we can just manage to wrest our dog from the authorities in Richmond and get him into her custody.

And Karin Grahn, Annie tells us, spent fifteen years as an animal control officer so she—unlike the three of us—actually knows something about the laws regarding impounding animals.

Karin Grahn will take Thiebaud, Annie says definitively. Karin Grahn will work with him, all this is simply what is now going to happen, so we can stop with the horror show Jack and I have been playing out in our minds.

The important thing is for Jack and me to not sit by and passively do nothing. Forget the neighbors who aren't our business anyway. We actually might want to pray for them since they have nothing to look forward to aside from living out their wretched little lives in their bleak little surfside mansion with their fleet of expensive cars.

What Jack and I are going to do is to demonstrate to all the various agencies involved how very seriously we are taking this matter. We will be giving this matter our full attention. We are going to acknowledge Thiebaud's truly terrible behavior. We will offer no excuses. We will take steps. The first step will be to have him signed up to go to Karin Grahn's by the time the animal control officer shows up at our house, maybe Karin will talk to them.

This is the way you'll get through this, Annie says. You will say you are taking corrective steps, then you'll go ahead and do exactly as you've said. You will follow the Good Orderly Direction.

The Good Orderly Direction is what Annie has to offer those of us who don't believe in God.

§
——

white shirt

——
§

Our dogs may be our last true link to Eden, writes Milan Kundera, as they seem to be ruled by neither evil nor jealousy—so all you and I may ever really know about paradise are those fleeting moments when we sit together, at peace, with our animals on the hillside that looks out over the glorious bay.

It was the night before our scheduled visit with animal control, Jack and I taking turns remembering that we have known paradise, trying to redream that vision and keep it alive for ourselves and for one another, the one keeping vigil as the other rested, each secretly listening for the sound of the truck arriving in the middle of the night with the people who'd wrest our dog from us, no questions asked, that moment when the three of us, as a family, would relinquish our last thin grasp on happiness.

So we three took turns slipping in and out of what was the one same dream and in my version my parents were both alive, both brothers too, and the forest floor was softly carpeted so you could lie down there and die with your dog beside you and in one of those sleep-wake interludes I noticed it was my dog now doing the dreaming, as Thiebaud's senses are in fact so much more vivid and alive than mine, and he does notice so much I never will, and remember all this with perfect accuity.

So it is in his memory Tee and I find ourselves at the top of our road in what is now a loud assault on the realm of the sensual: so many smells, all of them so loud it's like firecrackers going off all around us.

It's Thiebaud's dream, for sure, because Jack does not dream and I dream in Technicolor and in this one the hues and tints are all dimly shaded, darkly etched and shadowy, while the bold reek of skunk and sage, of wet and loamy earth, of manzanita, fox piss, dog shit, turkey scat, take on physical density as when you enter a spice bizarre, as we stand together at the bottom of the hill before beginning our trudge upward.

And now it's my dog leading me as we turn in past the locked park gate, ascending there at the holly, going up the trail to the top of the Knob by its shorter, steeper side.

And everything is still new to me and I'm in that exhaulted state of keen discovery, which is the real reason I love to move, that the new contains that element of sacred possibility, that we are alive again in this bright place where nothing yet is ruined, which means Jack and I have only just arrived in Point Richmond, and I've yet to get my bearings and am still so unsure but can become anyone I want, even the person for whom climbing this Knob is easy.

But not yet, as it is still one of the hardest things I've ever done, something I—in fact—cannot do, I cannot go on taking step after step, as it's like climbing five flights of stairs eight months pregnant and all I want to do is find a good enough excuse to stop or a place to sit down to rest or some reason to turn around and go home, telling myself I'll try again another day.

Thiebaud, though, is happy and romping, now racing in wider and wider circles, chasing through brambles, then into and out from beneath a thicket alive with small birds, now scrambling through the same pile of leaves again and again, as if to see a world made animate by his own disruption, and now he's digging in the soft-wet earth for voles, and is now at alert, all mud-faced and serious, watching the family of mismatched ravens, large as house cats, who sit on a dead tree branch unevenly spaced, squawking their serial caws down upon him as if declaiming the warning haiku my dog would do well to heed.

Then he's racing off around, tongue lolling, not caring if they're crows or ravens or whether the towhee's electric cry is from the spotted one or the treetop sitter they call a Western, my dog saying this world is MINE! is MINE! and as he chases and romps, I catch myself thinking: It's possible that I could be that happy too, and it is exactly here that my dog and I each lift our faces when we hear the first scream. It is a bloodcurdling scream and we hear it simultaneously.

A person is *screaming,* though it's the middle of the day, and there seems to be no reason, and this life-threatened scream carries far and wide, the scream that cannot be ignored, a call-911-type Kitty Genovese scream that demands everyone's attention, so you must react. If you don't react, you aren't alive, let alone a dog or a human person.

So my dog and I look upward to the top of the Knob where these screams are coming from and we see this very diminuitive person, tiny as a child, then discern that it's a small blonde woman who's standing there under the eucalyptus screaming down in our direction, which seems entirely odd and even unlikely as we're nearly half a football field's length away from her. Her screams seem to be directed at us, as if they're being made for us to hear, and my dog—his ears like Post-its, canted first forward, then back—looks at me like WTF? then discerns, before I can, what he must do. He's discovered the true cause of her terror: This woman's a runner, she's reached the top of the Knob ahead of whatever ghostly thing that's been chasing her, and my dog, with his only-big-enough-to-get-the-basics brain decides her fear is caused by the strange beast who's there on her heels obviously threatening her, and being the good dog Thiebaud is, he starts bounding up the trail as if he's Lassie in a TV show and he's on his way to save her.

But now the screaming woman, who's kept screaming all along, is screaming even louder and what she's screaming now filters down to us as words and what she saying is this:

KEEP THAT GODDAMNED THING AWAY FROM
FROM ME AND MY DOG!

ȣ ȣ ȣ

When the front-door buzzer rasps the next morning, it's at the civilized hour of nine fifteen. Jack and I are not only up and dressed, we've had a chance to rehearse the parts we've taken on and are now going to play.

We have each set out our individual jobs, have even practiced, as we do when we get home from our dance lessons. We are learning swing, and in this, as in swing, he's assigned the role of Lead while I will be the Follow. This does not mean that he is right and I am wrong, it means only that we've assigned leadership roles and I will behave exactly like the old-school Washington wife I never truly became and will nod in pleasant agreement, offering clarification only if this is asked of me. I will not interrupt to correct my husband, though his version of these events may be even *vastly wrong,* nor will I interject an anecdote that might lead this story down an altogether amusing but unnecessary byway. Instead, we have settled on One Main Version of These Events, and this is Jack's Version.

We have agreed that this time we will both be going by Jack's Version not because his version is more accurate, but because this will allow us to speak in one clear and coherent voice, which is simply way less confusing than what they have going on down the hill from us at Chomsky's house.

I will not interrupt him in his storytelling, even when Jack flubs a detail, his not being able to remember a name to save his life unless you are an obscure Japanese novelist or your name is Tomas Tranströmer or otherwise important to the Paradise Library. Jack's memory for names, particularly those of girls, particularly those of Blonde Girls of the Britney–Lindsay–Taylor Swift celebrity looka-like variety is so astonishingly bad that the year Eva was in fifth grade he gave up the bother of even trying and called each and every one of her friends "Tiffany." I will, however, not breathe a word of this or any other amusing biographical detail with the folks from animal control as these details are Off Topic. Instead, I vow to stay on task and refrain from wandering down any of the various narrative byways.

What Jack and I have decided is we must both be present to the officer and in no way fearful, as calm and Buddhistically confident as the screaming woman isn't, also bright and kind and rational, to provide a vivid contrast with the Bixbee-Medinas.

We open the door to Kim Fuentes, officer of Contra Costa County's Animal Services Department. She's there, she says, to investigate our dog's activity number 555-1212. It may be in answer to my lap-swimming prayers that Annie's God has sent us not just a woman but one whose face is kind and intelligent.

Jack and I ask her in. The three of us then go together to sit at the dining table. Our house this morning is tidy, visually coherent, in spite of the countless objects on display. These are arranged as altars and tableaux: like objects in any garden or museum, they must be carefully tended, which is Jack's job, not mine. Our dog—the dog Jack and I both recognize to be the Right Dog for us just as we understand ourselves to be this dog's Right People—is nowhere to be seen, but his messy dog toys are not strewn around. Obviously a neat dog lives here with two neat and coherent people.

That our house is neat and well-organized is something I can say without pride as I'm not the one responsible, though I'm probably given credit in that I'm a woman who works at home. I don't hold myself accountable for the way our house looks since I am not its steward. Our house person, that is, the one who actively *husbands* our household in the more ancient sense, is my own husband, Jack.

This is a clear division of labor based on aptitude, as he is good at domestic organization while I am not. If my memory is good at names and faces, for scenes that come complete with nine kinds of weather and encyclopedias of backstory and screenplays full of dialogue, his is the one in which mental lists reside, so he knows what we need and what we have on hand, so it is Jack who makes weekly trips to the Berkeley Bowl or to Tokyo Fish.

The morning of Officer Fuentes's visit, Jack and I have not hidden our dog from animal control, as had occurred to us. Instead we've done what was advised by Annie's wise counsel and are following a Good Orderly Direction: We have Taken Steps, having already called Karin Grahn, having already signed up Thiebaud to stay a week with her in Santa Rosa to try to get to the bottom of his aggressive behavior.

Tee's there on the bed in our bedroom, door closed to keep him from rushing up to greet Officer Fuentes too eagerly. The officer seems not only kind but even friendly. In fact, one of the first sentences out of her mouth is, *I've already been down the hill to speak to your neighbors, so now I think I ought to hear Thiebaud's side of the story.*

Thiebaud's side of the story, she says, and I am so shocked and grateful tears jolt to my eyes. I hadn't realized my dog even *got to have a side to this story!* I might have right here lurched into some disjointed telling of my version of last night's dream, which is actually a dim memory of something that really happened, how out of that dim and fall-fragrant air my dog had misread the cue and had misunderstood and thought he could be a hero and how he'd come to blame the old greyhound now for something that was neither dog's fault at all, but I don't. I don't say a word, as I am following the excellent advice of Ms. Lamott and Mr. Dickerson, and so I am sitting on every novelistic impulse I've ever possessed, that is, I do not elaborate. Instead, I nod pleasantly and am very, very quiet.

I'm quiet because we are sticking to our plan and it's Jack who's appointed to speak for us and so he does. He states his version of the facts with such complete conviction that I find all of it persuasive, even the parts I know to be either slightly skewed or even completely scrambled. I am being carried along by the story because the manner in which he tells it is so compelling, his ability to make all those complicated linkages both obvious and clear. His version is always nicer than mine. In Jack's kinder, more harmonious, a tad more storybook version of reality even our cartoon neighbors down the hill are generously included, so now he's telling Officer Fuentes that the Bixbee-Medinas have acted as they have because their dog is frail and old and they've been trying to protect him. Our neighbors are afraid they'll lose him, Jack says, adding that he and I know how that feels, that we too once had that happen to us and it was as bad a thing there is, just short of the other horrible things, too horrible to mention.

He tells her we're taking our dog's actions very seriously, that we've become so worried about our dog's behavior that we've arranged to send Thiebaud to the trainer for a week of behavior modification in the hope of dealing with this surprising aggression.

The deep sense of calm created by my husband's voice is so effecting that Officer Fuentes is entering into its peacefulness. Jack's calm voice is now saying: I see you, I hear you, I respect you, all of us here together are going to be able to handle this. We will deal with one another respectfully.

Jack tells Officer Fuentes Noah's version of that night in August almost a year and a half before. He tells her it's our suspicion that Mr. Bixbee actually struck his own dog when he was flailing at the two animals with his rake, or whatever it was, and here I refrain from adding the kinds of words I'd choose, such as *rain stick* or *cudgel*. For one thing, Jack says, it was an *L*-shaped tear and our own vet has told us a wound that shape is unusual in a dogfight.

True, she says, most dog bites result in puncture wounds, then Office Fuentes is once again bent over her clipboard, assiduously writing all this down.

When Jack says the words *our son*—not my wife's son or my stepson—but *our son*, taking on full ownership of Noah, just as he calls Eva *our daughter,* and Thiebaud *our dog*, I feel the muscles of my heart seize with a pulse of such joy and gratitude that my eyes fill again in awe at what we have accomplished. Come along with me, Jack once said. We'll raise these kids, we'll go some places and we'll do some things, we'll have fun, you'll see. We'll maybe take in a baseball game.

And I—who have trusted no one—did not rationally decide to go along with him, as this wasn't a rational decision. Why should I have trusted him? I didn't trust myself enough to know who I could even begin to trust.

But now I can see my husband intuitively trusting Officer Fuentes and he is telling her the backstory, how these two dogs have seemed—after that first fight so many months before—to have become the most virulent of enemies, an animus now exacerbated by Mr. Bixbee's habit of walking his dog off lead. Our neighbor allows Chomsky to simply wander anywhere he wants to go, Jack says, the man sometimes a block ahead or a block behind, this so our neighbor can ignore his animal as he pees or takes a dump on someone's lawn.

Some people feel it's beneath them to pick up after their animals,

Officer Fuentes says, and she writes all this down. Which is provocative behavior, she says, make no mistake. She looks up to make sure we take her point. People using their animals to act out aggressively is both cowardly and disrespectful and you will want to keep a camera or your phone handy so you can document this when you see it. This is so—if it ever comes to a hearing—you'll have evidence of Mr. Bixbee's behavior.

If it comes to a hearing, she has just said, her eyes crinkling as she smiles first at at Mr. Dickerson, then at me, and her meaning's clear: But do not worry, because this is *never going to happen*.

And you do want to get the dog in to see his own vet today, she goes on to say, so you'll have documentation of his injuries. This latest incident happened in the parks system, so it comes down to two dogs off lead in an off-lead area, so neither is at fault. Dogs fight. These things happen.

However, we are going to need to be extremely careful with your dog's records from here on to make sure there are no more write-ups. And I will need to get some pictures of the wounds on his face and head for his file so now might be a good time for me to meet the famous Mr. Thiebaud?

And we nod and it is here I go to fetch our dog from the bedroom.

Okay, I say to him aloud. You are going to act adult, all right? We all have to grow up sometime, do you hear me, Thiebaud? As hard as that might be. So I want none of your 10,000 Maniacs, okay? No getting crazy and hyper, no taking a quick lap around the dogtrack.

And I then clip on his short lead and Thiebaud walks calmly at heel down the hall with me, crosses the living room, and sits near us but not on top of us. He's panting, eyes almost closed, so it looks like he is smiling. He does seem proud of himself, like he's just won first place in the Good Dog Contest.

Officer Fuentes says, That's a good boy, Thiebaud, and rests her hand on his head to get him used to her, but he is already used to her, since they've been together forever in past incarnations and are experiencing *recognition,* so when she says to him, Okay, let's get a look at that awful gash of yours, it's in the soft voice of a true intimate.

She feels around to find the scabs of the places on his face and head where he was bitten, then takes a few pictures of the cut at the side of his mouth, now quickly healing, and Thiebaud, grateful for any and all attention, leans his full weight against her knees and rests his face in her lap and stares up at her adoringly and is already half asleep so Officer Fuentes has to lean over and whisper as she speaks to him:

Man, Thiebaud, why'd you want to go and get in all this trouble?

≈ ≈ ≈

To sit with a dog on a hillside on a glorious afternoon just might be enough for Jack and me. It was almost exactly that that he seemed to promise when he asked me to come away with him.

We were standing together on a cliff on Highway 1 by the side of his car, overlooking the Pacific, when he gestured with a sweep of his hand, saying, Not bad, huh? We stood on that windswept precipice, right there too on the precipice of falling in love.

But why should I trust you? I asked, not saying it aloud, When I've never trusted anyone?

Because I believe in you, Jane, Jack said. Then he smiled, turned to me and added, And I have excellent taste in people.

And I did trust him and I still do and time that had turned glacial now began again to move and Officer Fuentes, who trusted us, wrote up the incident for her sergeant, calling the two dogs equally culpable and our dog's file, marked PDA, was—as Jack and I imagined—put on a wobbly stack in some crammed back office buried deeply in a drawer marked Pending, as we never heard from any of those people again.

And true to our word we sent Thiebaud for a week of retooling with Karin Grahn, who explained what she thought we needed to know about our dog's psychology, that is, he's a good and willing dog with a cheerful temperment who's about exactly as smart as a dog like this would need to be, which is, not very. What this means is that we're the ones who have the responsibility in this regard, we're the ones in charge, and we need to behave like we know what we are doing so our dog doesn't have to. His judgment is poor, Karin Grahn said, witness his threat assessment of that one particular greyhound.

⚜ ⚜ ⚜

"There is a moment in a story in which the presence of grace can be felt as it waits to be accepted or rejected," wrote Flannery O'Connor, and here is what I remember of the first day of our story, the story Jack might call *Us, Excellent.*

It's noon, Jack's come home from work in the middle of the day to meet me at his house. He's taken his suit coat off, his dress shirt is blindingly white in the sunshine that floods in from the windows to the west beyond him. I see him as I come up onto the porch and look in through the open doorway. I've never been to his house before, which is found by climbing seventy-five stone steps up from the North Berkeley street below.

I see him through the door he's left standing open as he came in, half turned away from me, eyes down, sorting through his mail. Behind him is a fish tank that occupies almost the entire wall of the kitchen. The water's cloudy and through this dim water, bright carp swim in patches of gold and yellow and orange.

I am thinking of the heat of his hands and the smell of his neck and the soft pressure of his fingertips, matters I do not yet know but am here, evidently, to learn about and am noticing how—because I may have come here to break off this thing of ours before it has even become a thing—he remains concentrated on his mail and does not yet raise his eyes to me. He is a man, as I already know, of deep and remarkable concentration.

I already know this about him though I really don't know him at all. I know him so well I understand our future is already certain, that this future will be made clear to each of us the moment he lifts his face and looks at me. He will read our future in my eyes and his expression will then show me what I've said.

sources

Bradshaw, John. *Dog Sense: How the New Science of Dog Behavior Can Make a Better Friend to Your Pet* (New York: Basic Books, 2011).

Horowitz, Alexandra. *Inside of a Dog: What Dogs See, Smell and Know.* (New York, Scribner, 2010).

Yamazaki, Tetsu and Toyoharu, Kojima, Eds. *Legacy of the Dog: The Ultimate Illustrated Guide to over 200 Breeds.* (San Francisco Chronicle Books, 1993).

acknowledgments

My gratitude to my Birthday Friends on both coasts, who loved and sustained me and have listened to my stories. Thanks too to those in our large and complicated family, who've generously offered me these stories with the understanding that it is always only my version I'll ever be able to tell.

Alice Powers, Susan Bobst and Victoria Patterson each helped by reading early drafts of this book. Susan Clements typed the manuscript.

I am thankful for the insights of Elise Capron, the most wise and encouraging of agents.

For the editorial and production guidance from those at Counterpoint, particularly Dan Smetanka and Kelly Winton, I am deeply grateful.

And because it is our animals who make us more fully human by staying with us even when they've gone, I want to say their names: Gray, Phoebe, Mickey, Whitney, Rascal, Rusty, Dostoyevski, Coltrane, Gracie, Baccus, Michu, Reggie, Muffin, Sherpa, Puccini, and yup, you too, Jessica.

Father Church, the Episcopal priest who confirmed me, once told me dogs weren't to be found in heaven because, as he explained it, they do not have souls, but, Whistler? What does that ass know?